Y0-CDH-780

THE GOOD LIFE

THE GOOD LIFE

Unifying the Philosophy and Psychology of Well-Being

Michael A Bishop

OXFORD
UNIVERSITY PRESS

Oxford University Press is a department of the University of Oxford.
It furthers the University's objective of excellence in research, scholarship,
and education by publishing worldwide.

Oxford New York
Auckland Cape Town Dar es Salaam Hong Kong Karachi
Kuala Lumpur Madrid Melbourne Mexico City Nairobi
New Delhi Shanghai Taipei Toronto

With offices in
Argentina Austria Brazil Chile Czech Republic France Greece
Guatemala Hungary Italy Japan Poland Portugal Singapore
South Korea Switzerland Thailand Turkey Ukraine Vietnam

Oxford is a registered trade mark of Oxford University Press
in the UK and certain other countries.

Published in the United States of America by
Oxford University Press
198 Madison Avenue, New York, NY 10016

© Oxford University Press 2015

First issued as an Oxford University Press paperback, 2016

All rights reserved. No part of this publication may be reproduced,
stored in a retrieval system, or transmitted, in any form or by any means,
without the prior permission in writing of Oxford University Press,
or as expressly permitted by law, by license, or under terms agreed with the
appropriate reproduction rights organization. Inquiries concerning reproduction
outside the scope of the above should be sent to the Rights Department,
Oxford University Press, at the address above.

You must not circulate this work in any other form
and you must impose this same condition on any acquirer.

Library of Congress Cataloging-in-Publication Data
Bishop, Michael A
The good life : unifying the philosophy and psychology of well-being / Michael A Bishop.
p. cm.
Includes bibliographical references and index.
ISBN 978-0-19-992311-3 (hardcover); 978-0-19-060380-9 (paperback)
1. Well-being. 2. Positive psychology. I. Title.
BF575.H27B547 2015
170'.44—dc23
2014021211

For Taita

CONTENTS

Acknowledgments | ix
Note to Readers | xi

Introduction | 1

1. The Network Theory of Well-Being | 7

2. The Inclusive Approach to the Study of Well-Being | 14

3. Positive Causal Networks and the Network Theory
   of Well-Being | 35

4. Positive Causal Networks and Positive Psychology | 59

5. The Case for the Network Theory: An Inference to the Best
   Explanation | 108

6. Issues in the Psychology of Happiness and Well-Being | 149

7. Objections to the Network Theory | 184

8. Conclusion | 208

REFERENCES | 213
INDEX | 231

ACKNOWLEDGMENTS

I have benefited greatly from presenting earlier versions of this material to the following audiences:

- The Symposium on Naturalism in Science, Kansas State University
- The Ethical and Social Scientific Perspectives on Well-Being, California State University, Long Beach
- The First Colombian Conference in Logic, Epistemology, and Philosophy of Science, Universidad de los Andes
- The Summer Institute for Bounded Rationality, the Max Planck Institute for Human Development, Berlin, Germany
- Instituto de Investigaciones Filosóficas, Universidad Nacional Autónoma de México (UNAM), Mexico City, Mexico
- The Moral Philosophy Research Group, Washington University at St. Louis
- Philosophy Department Colloquium, Union College
- The 7th International Symposium of Cognition, Logic and Communication: Morality and the Cognitive Sciences, Riga, Latvia

Many colleagues, friends, and students have been generous in helping me with this book. Valerie Tiberius and Steve McFarlane gave me detailed and thoughtful comments on the entire manuscript. This book would be much poorer but for their generosity. I owe a special debt to Joe Mendola, who showed me how to improve the section on normativity while wisely ignoring my repeated and strenuous insistence that I was *done* with the book. I want to thank Daniel Haybron, J. D. Trout, Sam Wren-Lewis, Steve Downes, and Jack Justus for giving me valuable feedback on significant portions of the manuscript. In conversation, the comments and sometimes pointed objections of Francesco Orsi, Stephen Stich, Clifford Sosis, Timothy Schroeder, David Fajardo-Chica, John Doris, and Walter Sinnott-Armstrong forced me to rethink my views and arguments. So many good people have helped me clarify my thoughts on these topics that I cannot hope to mention them all. But I would be remiss not to thank Anna Alexandrova, Erik Angner, Lorraine Besser-Jones, Sarah Chant, Paul Churchland, Heather Cipolletti, Daniel Cohnitz, Fiery Cushman, Gabriel De Marco, Adam Feltz, Abraham Graber, Joshua Greene, Soren Haggqvist, Gilbert Harman, Philip Kitcher, Joshua Knobe, Randy Larsen, James Lesher, Edouard Machery, Maximiliano Martinez, Maria Merritt, Dominic Murphy, Shaun Nichols, Jesse Prinz, Jason Raibley, Peter Railton, Stephanie Rocknak, Richard Samuels, Chandra Sripada, Michael Strevens, Charles Wallis, and Susan Wolf.

I would like to express my appreciation to the production team at Oxford University Press for their excellent work putting this book into production. And finally, I would like to thank Lucy Randall for her light, astute editorial touch and for graciously shepherding me through the publication process.

NOTE TO READERS

For those who want to understand the views in this book well enough to get through a cocktail conversation, I recommend reading the 16 or so pages that make up the introduction, first chapter, and conclusion. For those who wish to understand the views well enough to be able to dismiss them in good conscience, just the conclusion will do.

Inclusive:
containing a
specified element
as part of a
whole

Stalemate: Any position
or situation in which
no action can be taken
or progress made.
(deadlock)

Both study "wellbeing"
but, the views on how to
get there or achieve
are different
(2) problems
(1) solution

Introduction

Philosophers and psychologists study well-being. And each group is saddled with its own peculiar problems. The philosophers, despite their many insights, are in a never-ending stalemate. And the psychologists, despite their many results, are incapable of providing a clear account of their discipline, Positive Psychology. The study of well-being has followed the outlines of a frivolous Hollywood romantic comedy. The young lovers "meet cute" in ancient Greece. But when psychology goes experimental in the nineteenth century, irreconcilable differences end their courtship. They part, each one alone, sadder, and in denial about how essential the other was to their success. Will the star-crossed lovers persist with their foolishness and continue their lonely struggles? Or will they resolve their differences, reunite dramatically, music swelling in the background—okay, enough. To understand this book, just know that I'm a sucker for the Hollywood ending.

The secret to getting the Hollywood ending, to resolving the stalemate for the philosophers and finding a secure foundation for the psychologists, is right under your nose. It's the first sentence of this page. The idea behind the inclusive approach to the study of well-being, the approach I'll be defending in this book,

Thesis

1

is that if both philosophers and psychologists study well-being, then well-being—the real thing, whatever it is—will express itself in their labors. To discover the nature of well-being, we must begin with the assumption that both philosophers and scientists are roughly right about well-being, and then figure out what it is they're *all* roughly right about. (They can't all be exactly right. There's too much disagreement.)

The inclusive approach gives us two simple tests for knowing when we have found the correct theory of well-being: When philosophers build their various accounts of well-being, the true theory will imply that they are all successfully describing *well-being*, even if they have some of the details wrong. And when psychologists use their various methods to study well-being, the true theory will imply that they are all studying *well-being*, even if they have some of the details wrong. The true theory will explain how philosophers and psychologists, despite their sometimes dramatic disagreements, have been studying the same thing—well-being—all this time. If this approach strikes you as problematic, ask yourself: Where *else* would you begin to try to discover the nature of well-being but with the best research done by philosophers and scientists on the subject? Given the serious troubles facing the lone philosopher and the lone psychologist, we cannot rely on just one of them. We need the Hollywood ending.

Consider first the philosopher's plight. Three theories of well-being dominate the philosophical landscape: hedonism, Aristotelianism, and the informed desire theory. The basic idea behind hedonism is that your well-being is a function of the balance of your pleasure over your pain. It is the James Brown ("I feel good!") theory of well-being. The gist of Aristotle's view is that well-being involves having a virtuous character that promotes your flourishing—an active, healthy engagement with the world. It is the Chuck Berry ("Johnny B. Goode") theory of

(Agreeing to Agree)

need ingredients to make a cate one does not exist without the other well-being. And the informed desire theory holds that well-being involves getting what you want, usually on the assumption that you're properly rational and informed. It is the Mick Jagger ("You can't always get what you want") theory of well-being.

No contemporary philosopher argues for or against any of these theories by appealing to science, to the results psychologists have unearthed about well-being. Now, it's true that most philosophers couldn't have paid attention to the science, as philosophers have been at this for millennia and psychologists for mere decades. But most philosophers today would argue that the problem isn't that psychologists are so late to the party. The problem is that science is *incapable* of delivering evidence that could confirm or disconfirm a philosophical theory about well-being. Their argument for ignoring science goes something like this: "Take any scientific discovery that purports to be about well-being. Whether or not it really is about well-being depends on what well-being is. And it is philosophy that tells us what well-being is. To have a philosophical theory of well-being rely on scientific evidence would be to put the cart before the horse."

This disavowal of scientific evidence has a serious consequence. It leaves philosophers with only their own considered judgments about well-being to serve as evidence for their theories. And different philosophers have different considered judgments. Some philosophers have broadly hedonistic judgments, others have broadly Aristotelian judgments, and yet others have judgments that follow the contours of the informed desire theory. So while philosophers will sometimes agree that some particular version of (say) hedonism is false, as long as there are enough clever philosophers whose commonsense judgments are broadly hedonistic, hedonism will survive. Philosophers are masters at developing coherent theories that answer to their own opinions. So as long as there is a broad diversity in the commonsense judgments of philosophers, theoretical consensus will remain a pipe dream. The inclusive approach breaks this stalemate by making our theories answer to more than just philosophers' considered judgments.

Psychologists who study happiness and well-being face a related problem. Their discipline, often called Positive Psychology, appears to be a giant hodgepodge. It has no agreed upon definition. For example, two leaders of the field offer a characterization that is a list of 26 items Positive Psychology is "about." The list includes satisfaction, courage, aesthetic sensibility, spirituality, wisdom, nurturance, moderation, and work ethic (Seligman and Csikszentmihalyi 2000, 5). The authors do not explain how they drew up this list. Why does spirituality make it but not pleasure? Perhaps there is a reason—and perhaps the reason is just that no such list could be complete. But we might see this loose characterization and worry that Positive Psychology is not a principled, well-defined scientific discipline, but a research program built on the subjective views of some psychologists about the right way to live.

To properly address this worry, psychologists must engage with philosophy, but not *only* with the philosophical literature on well-being. That literature, as I pointed out a couple paragraphs back, is too fragmented to provide Positive Psychology with a solid foundation. What Positive Psychology needs is a bit of fairly conventional philosophy of science. Philosophy of science is a branch of philosophy that seeks to understand particular scientific theories or disciplines (e.g., How should we interpret quantum mechanics? What is biological fitness?) as well as some basic features of science in general (e.g., What is the relationship between theory and evidence? Does science make progress? And if so, what is the nature of that progress?). If we start with some fairly uncontroversial assumptions about how science works, we can stitch together the methods of science and philosophy to form an inclusive approach to the study of well-being. And then we can use this approach to resolve the stalemate problem for philosophers and the foundation problem for psychologists.

Positive Psychology has attracted a lot of attention because of its potential to offer practical advice backed by science. It can tell individuals, institutions, and governments that some activity or policy is likely to promote well-being. Such recommendations have raised two families of objections. The first is evidential. Practical advice must be supported by strong evidence. Will the proposed activity or policy really bring about the desired result? Will it be effective only for some people but not others? Will it backfire and harm some people? Every thoughtful proponent of Positive Psychology recognizes the importance of addressing this evidential worry. But it is not the topic of this book.

The second line of argument against the recommendations derived from Positive Psychology is a philosophical one: If Positive Psychology makes recommendations, and it does, then it must be in the business of promoting *something*. Some critics think we should shun Positive Psychology because it promotes a delusional optimism-at-all-costs attitude. Others decry Positive Psychology as assuming a superficial form of hedonism that promotes shallow happy feelings at the expense of deeper, more enduring goods. Yet others see accounts of Positive Psychology that embrace characteristics that not everyone deems valuable—such as work ethic or spirituality—and they come to believe that the discipline is built on a provincial, moralistic conception of the good life. These interpretations may be uncharitable, but the lack of a clear explanation of what Positive Psychology is about opens it up to this criticism. If Positive Psychology is not in the business of promoting delusional optimism or Dudley Do-Right morality, then what is it promoting?

My contention is that Positive Psychology rests on a plausible and attractive conception of well-being. It is essential for us to get clear about this. Because before we can know how strenuously to pursue well-being, or even whether to pursue it at all, we need to know what well-being is. That is what this book is about.

Thesis of Book [handwritten margin note]

Chapter 1

The Network Theory of Well-Being

I want to describe the network theory of well-being as I might to a friend or sibling: simply, succinctly and with no theoretical fuss. I will not try to satisfy the nattering critic that sits on my shoulder, or yours. We'll have the rest of the book to deal with them. A good way to start is with an exercise. How would you explain that a person has a high degree of well-being without actually using the word "well-being" or its synonyms? If you aren't already corrupted by a philosophical theory, you might offer a thumbnail sketch like this: "Felicity is in a happy and fulfilling committed relationship, she has close and caring friends, she keeps fit by playing tennis, a sport she enjoys, and her professional life is both successful and satisfying." Most people's description will include both objective and subjective facts about the person. These facts include:

1. positive feelings, moods, emotions (e.g., joy, contentment),
2. positive attitudes (e.g., optimism, hope, openness to new experiences),
3. positive traits (e.g., friendliness, curiosity, perseverance), and

4. accomplishments (e.g., strong relationships, professional success, fulfilling hobbies or projects).

So far, so good. But how does this ramshackle set of facts fit into a coherent whole? How are we supposed to unite them into a coherent theory of well-being? The answer I propose is simple: We don't have to. The world has already joined them together in a web of cause and effect. The network theory holds that to have well-being is to be "stuck" in a self-perpetuating cycle of positive emotions, positive attitudes, positive traits, and successful engagement with the world.

Felicity's well-being is not an accidental conglomeration of happy facts. These states—her committed relationship, her friendships, her exercise regimen, her professional success, her confidence and sense of mastery, her joie de vivre, her friendliness, her moxie and adventurousness, her curiosity, her hope and optimism—build upon and foster one another, forming a kind of causal web or network. A person high in well-being is in a positive cycle or "groove." Take any fact that is part of Felicity's well-being, say, her professional success. It is caused by other facts that make up Felicity's well-being—her curiosity, moxie, optimism, and confidence, her exercise regimen, her social support. And it is also a cause of some of those facts. Her professional success bolsters her income, her optimism, her confidence, and the strength of her relationships. Felicity's professional success is a node in a causal network of facts that make up part of her well-being (Figure 1.1). What is true of Felicity's professional success is also true of other components of her well-being. Each is embedded in a causal web of positive feelings, positive attitudes, positive traits, and accomplishments.

An important feature of Figure 1.1 is that certain states (her optimism, confidence, and social support) both strengthen and are strengthened by her professional success. Felicity's well-being

FIGURE 1.1

Professional Success as a Node in a Positive Causal Network

consists of some cyclical processes (Figure 1.2). Her professional success leads her to acquire, maintain, or strengthen other positive features of her person; and in turn these positive features help foster her professional success; and so on.

Many elements of well-being involve such positive cycles. For example, Felicity's optimism helps her overcome challenges and makes her more successful socially and professionally, and having success tends to bolster Felicity's optimism (Seligman 1990). Felicity's friendships and committed relationship provide her with various kinds of material and psychological support, which help to make Felicity more trusting, more extraverted,

FIGURE 1.2

A Positive Professional Success Cycle

and more generous, and these traits in turn make Felicity a better friend and partner, which tend to strengthen her friendships and relationship (Fredrickson 1998). Felicity's exercise regimen gives her more strength, energy, and positive emotions, which contribute to her ability to continue her exercise regimen. And so on.

A person high in well-being has positive emotions, attitudes, traits, and accomplishments that form an interlocking web of states that build and feed on each other. According to the network theory, the state of well-being is the state of being in (or, to use philosopher's jargon, *instantiating*) a positive causal network. Someone not in a *state* of well-being might nonetheless have a more modest degree of well-being. She might have some positive feelings, attitudes, traits, or successes, but not enough to kick-start a full-blown, self-perpetuating causal web of positivity. Such a person would instantiate a *fragment* of a positive causal network.

To speak of a positive causal network is not just a fancy way to say success breeds success. The child of privilege who achieves consistent success largely as a result of being given advantages unavailable to others does not necessarily have well-being. The same holds for the entrepreneur who leverages her current wealth to amass even greater wealth. The success inherent in well-being must be the result of a particular sort of process— one that essentially involves positive emotions, attitudes, and traits. It may be that the privileges of wealth and power make it easier to attain well-being. But well-being does not simply involve being caught up in a "success breeds success" cycle. It is more colloquially captured by the idea that we sometimes find ourselves in a positive groove, or in the zone, or riding high. Of course, the feeling that we're "cookin' with gas" is not a sure sign that we have well-being. But it captures the intuitive idea behind the network theory.

Compare/ contrast

What can cause depression

network theory

(2) Parts

Some have it some don't

Another way to understand positive causal networks is to contrast them with negative or vicious ones. Think about a time in your life when you were blue or down. Even if your episode did not meet the standard diagnostic criteria for an affective disorder, any memorable blue period will include some of the characteristic features of dysthymia—depressed mood, diminished interest or pleasure in activities, loss of energy, feelings of worthlessness, excessive or inappropriate guilt, morbid thoughts, indecisiveness, diminished ability to think or concentrate, insomnia or hypersomnia, psychomotor agitation or retardation, and impaired functioning. What makes dysthymia particularly cruel is that its features are links in self-maintaining causal cycles. Negative thoughts, feelings, attitudes, behaviors, and dysfunctions causally build upon and reinforce one another. A deep melancholy can lead to life problems at school, at work, and in friendships and relationships, and these life problems can in turn produce greater feelings of melancholy and despair, which can in turn produce more life problems. Anyone who has suffered through a deep blue period, much less a serious depression, will not need to be convinced of the grim reality of such vicious cycles. Positive cycles can be plausibly understood as their mirror image.

Let's recap. The network theory has two parts. The state of well-being is the state of being in a positive causal network. But a person might have some degree of well-being even without a full-blown positive causal network. Sad Steve's life might go better for him because he has friends who genuinely care about him, even though he is not in a state of well-being. To say that a state (or set of states) is a *fragment* of a positive causal network is to say that it could be a significant link in a positive causal network for that person, keeping relatively constant the sort of person he is (i.e., his personality, his goals and his general dispositions). So a person's degree of well-being is determined by

(a) the strength of her positive causal network and (b) the strength of her positive causal network fragments.

These are the basic elements of the network theory. I want to highlight three of its features.

1. *Well-being is a real condition.* It is as real as being depressed or having the flu. A person's well-being consists of both subjective and objective facts about a person. A challenge for any theory of well-being is how to stitch these disparate facts together into a coherent whole. The network theory connects them in a simple and natural way, in the way the world connects them: with causal bonds.

2. *Well-being is causally stable.* It is a condition that in reasonably favorable conditions tends to perpetuate itself. Positive states tend to bring about further positive states. Of course, well-being and its component processes are neither permanent nor inevitable. A central project in the study of well-being is to learn about the dynamics of positive causal networks. There are factors, both environmental and internal to the person, that can frustrate or extinguish positive causal networks. And there are things we can do to establish, maintain, and strengthen them.

3. *Well-being is multiply realizable.* The network theory provides a smooth, unified explanation for why the professional athlete and the spritely octogenarian might both have a high degree of well-being even though the details of their lives are very different. In both cases, their well-being consists of a dynamic state of self-maintaining causal links among positive feelings, emotions, attitudes, traits, and accomplishments.

At this point, the nattering critic on my shoulder—and I suspect the nattering critic on your shoulder—will not be silenced.

What evidence is there for believing the network theory? What is it for a feeling, emotion, attitude, or trait to be *positive*? And what is it for someone to be *successfully* engaged with the world? How can the network theory account for the graded nature of well-being? Can it explain what makes well-being good or valuable? These difficult questions fall outside the scope of this short, intuitive chapter.

Chapter 2

The Inclusive Approach to the Study of Well-Being

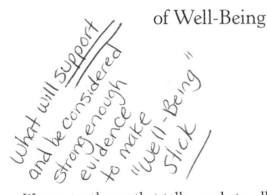

What will support and be considered strong enough evidence to make "Well-Being" Stick

We want a theory that tells us what well-being is. How are we to arrive at such a theory? What evidence should we consider? And how should we proceed from that evidence? Getting clear about these methodological questions is important. If we aren't clear about what counts as evidence, we can't be clear about what counts as a strong case for a theory. If the true theory doesn't need to account for the findings of science, we can safely ignore the science. If it must account for our commonsense judgments about well-being, then we'd better pay close attention to those judgments. What's more, our methods inevitably bind us to substantive assumptions about what we're investigating. We adopt a method for investigating well-being because we think that it is a good way to learn about it. But whether it is a good way to learn about well-being depends on what well-being is. We bump up against a form of Meno's Paradox: We can't learn about something unless we already know what it is. To discover what well-being is, we need a plan for finding out about it; but such a plan inevitably makes substantive assumptions about what well-being is. This conundrum is not a reason to doubt our ability to figure out what well-being is. Nor is it a reason to start with timid assumptions in the hope of minimizing our risk of failure. The meek might inherit the earth, but they seldom get far in philosophy. The best we can do is put our starting points out there and be clear-eyed about the risks we're assuming.

[handwritten: Containing a specified element as part of a whole]

1. The Inclusive Approach to the Study of Well-Being

The core of the inclusive approach is the assumption that philosophers, scientists, and laypeople are generally successful in talking about and identifying instances of well-being. Most of us have some firsthand experience with well-being, and so we have a reasonably good sense of what tends to bring it about, what it feels like, and what it comprises. While people make mistakes about well-being, even systematic ones, the inclusive approach begins with an assumption of basic respect. When philosophers theorize about well-being, they're usually not too far from the truth about it. When psychologists study well-being, they usually manage to successfully investigate it. By the same token, when laypeople talk about well-being, they usually manage to successfully refer to it. This basic respect assumption has two large virtues. First, it is hard to see where else to begin our study. If philosophers or psychologists or laypeople are deeply confused about well-being, that should be the end point—not the starting point—of our investigation into the nature of well-being. Second, the basic respect assumption is bound to bear fruit whether it's true or false. If it's true, this will give us a large base of evidence on which to build a theory, much larger, as we shall see, than the traditional approach envisions. If it's false, the best way to find out is to assume it's true and test it. If the assumption gets us into trouble, if it leads to

[handwritten margin note: Two things had to be same but differently]

(margin handwritten notes: "3 theses", "3 approaches that need to be considered when what well-being's really is seeking to find out what well-being's really is")

contradiction or incoherence, trying to discover the best way out of the trouble is bound to produce interesting results. Are philosophers off-base in their theorizing about well-being? Are psychologists deceived in thinking they are studying and learning about well-being? Are laypeople failing to talk about or reliably track well-being? There is good reason to think that the basic respect assumption will bear fruit, even if it's false—in fact, especially if it's false!

The most natural way to spell out the basic respect assumption—or better, what I find the most natural way to spell it out—is in terms of three basic theses. The first is that well-being is a real condition that people talk about, philosophers theorize about, and psychologists study. The second is that we should begin our investigation by adopting a strident modesty about the accuracy of our commonsense judgments about well-being. They are reasonably accurate, neither deeply mistaken nor perfectly true. Of course, this might be false. But deep skepticism or unbridled optimism about our commonsense judgments should be the outcome of our investigation into well-being, not the starting point of that investigation. Third, and most controversially, the evidential base for a theory of well-being— the evidence that a theory should explain—includes both scientific findings and commonsense judgments about well-being.

1.1. Well-Being Is a Real Condition

If well-being is something that philosophers can theorize about, that psychologists can investigate, and that laypeople can successfully talk about, then it would seem that well-being is real. It is like being depressed or having the flu. It is a state or condition in which a person can find herself, a condition that scientists can learn about, and that people can talk about, perhaps imperfectly, when we talk about well-being. If well-being is something psychologists can study, then it must be a reasonably stable condition that can be identified and characterized by standard empirical methods.

1.2. Moderate Epistemic Modesty

relating to knowledge or to the degree of its validation

If well-being is a real state, we should begin our inquiry into its nature with a stridently moderate attitude about the accuracy of our commonsense judgments about it. We cannot start off overly skeptical, thinking that our everyday judgments are all wrong, or overly reverential, thinking that they are perfect. Of course, the conclusion we should ultimately accept regarding the quality of our commonsense judgments about well-being will depend on the outcome of our investigation. Behind this epistemic modesty is an important and widely accepted assumption about how we understand, talk about, and investigate states or conditions (or, in philosopher's jargon, *kinds*). We can talk about them even when we're quite ignorant or mistaken about their real nature (Kripke 1972, Putnam 1975). People who had deeply mistaken or incomplete views about the nature of water, electricity, electrons, atoms, planets, stars, meteors, asteroids, combustion, disease, light (this list could go on and on) were nonetheless able to talk about and refer to those things. The inclusive approach is not committed to any bold philosophical assumption about the nature of kinds or how we refer to them. It is committed only to the very weak assumption that well-being is a condition we can refer to even if we're somewhat ignorant or mistaken about its real nature.

What happens if it should turn out that our commonsense judgments about well-being are systematically mistaken— that most of what we believe about well-being is false? In that case, the inclusive approach, like any approach that assumes that our pretheoretical judgments are at least somewhat

Judgements

accurate, will fail. Perhaps we conclude that, like vampires or perpetual motion machines, well-being doesn't exist. Or perhaps we conclude that, like vehicle or fruit, well-being is a very broad category that encompasses many different kinds of thing. Either result would be interesting. Frankly, I was hoping for one of these dramatic results when I began this project. But as it happens, I believe there exists a real condition that psychologists study and that answers reasonably well to our commonsense judgments about well-being. But I'm getting ahead of myself.

1.3. The Role of Scientific Evidence

The modesty about our commonsense judgments implicit in the inclusive approach has important implications for how to properly study well-being—or rather, how *not* to study it. It tells us that we cannot start our investigation by taking our everyday judgments for granted as our *only* primary source of evidence. But that leaves the inclusive approach with a puzzle: What other source of evidence is a theory of well-being supposed to explain? Perhaps science. At first blush, however, this suggestion is unpromising. No empirical study can directly confirm or disconfirm a philosophical theory about the nature of well-being. As Daniel Haybron notes with respect to theories of happiness: "What kind of empirical study could possibly tell us which account [of happiness] is correct? One might as well try performing an experiment to determine whether water is H_2O or a kind of bicycle" (2003, 312). If science can't serve as a source of evidence, then it seems that common sense is the only evidence we have left. Perhaps this is not ideal. But it's better than nothing.

Before settling for common sense as our only substantive source of evidence, let's revisit the basic respect assumption: There is a real condition, W, that laypeople talk about, that philosophers theorize about, and that psychologists investigate. This provides three checks on whether W is well-being.

1. Common sense: the assumption that W is well-being (and thus that "well-being" refers to W) makes most of our considered, everyday judgments about well-being true or approximately true.
2. Philosophy: the assumption that W is well-being makes most philosophical theories about the nature of well-being true or approximately true.
3. Science: the assumption that W is well-being makes it true that the empirical study of well-being is the study of W or phenomena related to W.

Since contemporary philosophical theories rely on common-sense intuitions as their primary source of evidence (more on this soon), we can combine (1) and (2). And so the inclusive approach identifies two sources of evidence for a theory about the nature of well-being, common sense and science.

The inclusive approach requires that the case for a theory of well-being be made on standard scientific grounds. The argument will be an abductive one—an inference to the best explanation. What is the best explanation for the fact that psychological research on what we intuitively deem to be well-being is about W and that most of our commonsense judgments about well-being seem to be true or approximately true about W? The best explanation is that W is, in fact, well-being. The case for a theory of well-being will not consist of deductive arguments derived from pure reason to conclusions presumed to be necessarily true. What's more, showing that a theory yields some counterintuitive consequences is not, by itself, going to be particularly damning. The reason to accept a theory of well-being is that it organizes a wide range of otherwise diverse evidence from both science and common sense.

2. The Traditional Approach to the Study of Well-Being

The traditional philosophical approach to the study of well-being encompasses two theses. The Descriptive Adequacy condition holds that the most important demand on a theory of well-being is that it should capture our commonsense judgments. And the Philosophy First assumption holds that the philosophical study of the nature of well-being is logically prior to any scientific findings about well-being. The main problem with the traditional approach is that it begins with an exceptionally high degree of faith in the quality of our commonsense judgments about well-being. It assumes that they are so accurate that they should serve as the primary source of evidence for a theory of well-being. A striking way to frame this epistemological over-optimism is in terms of the diversity challenge: Different people have different commonsense judgments about well-being. How are we to choose among them? While the proponent of the traditional approach has a number of potential replies to this challenge, my claim is not that the traditional approach is doomed. My claim is that the over-optimism of the traditional approach is a serious enough worry to motivate trying something new.

2.1. Descriptive Adequacy

The Descriptive Adequacy condition holds that the most important source of evidence that a theory of well-being must account for is our ordinary, commonsense judgments. James Griffin states that "the notion we are after is the ordinary notion of 'well-being'" (1986, 10). In L. W. Sumner's discussion of what we want from a theory of welfare, which he takes to be "more or less the same" as well-being (1996, 1), he concisely articulates the first part of the traditional approach:

[T]he best theory about the nature of [well-being] is the one which is most faithful to our ordinary concept and our ordinary experience. That experience is given by what we think or feel or know about well-being, both our own and that of others. The data which a candidate theory must fit, therefore, consist of the prodigious variety of our preanalytic convictions (1996, 10–11).

The degree of fit between a theory of well-being and our pretheoretic convictions is "a function of the extent to which the truth conditions [the theory] offers can support and systematize our intuitive assessments." While Sumner does not argue that descriptive adequacy is the sole requirement that the correct theory of well-being must satisfy, it is the most important. It is "the basic test" (1996, 10). Valerie Tiberius has also embraced the Descriptive Adequacy condition:

Formal analyses [which provide an account of the nature of well-being] are to be evaluated on the basis of how well they accommodate our uses of the concept in question and how well they fit with our ordinary experience. In other words, formal accounts of well-being are evaluated primarily in terms of their descriptive adequacy. The most descriptively adequate account of well-being is the one that is most faithful to our pre-philosophical convictions about well-being (2004, 299).

So a theory that tells us about the nature of well-being must be "faithful" to our everyday judgments about well-being.

The Descriptive Adequacy condition holds that our convictions about well-being serve as the primary arbiters, the primary evidence, for our theories of well-being. "We manifest these convictions whenever we judge that our lives are going well or badly, that pursuing some objective will be profitable or advantageous for us, that a change in our circumstances has left us better or worse off, that some policy would enhance or erode our quality of life, that some measure is necessary in order to protect the interest of our family or community, that a practice which is beneficial for us may be harmful to others, that we are enjoying a higher standard of living than our forebears, and so on" (Sumner 1996, 11). And yet, Sumner rightly notes that philosophers have "no special expertise" when it comes to telling "us what is good or bad for us, or [advising] us on how to attain the former and avoid the latter" (1996, 7). There appears to be a tension here. On the one hand, philosophers have "no special expertise" about "what is good or bad for us." On the other hand, philosophers' convictions implicit in judgments like "our lives are going well or badly" are so accurate and so worthy of belief that they constitute the primary evidence for theories of well-being. How can this be?

The solution to this tension involves distinguishing between judgments about the *nature* of well-being and judgments about the *causes, effects, and correlates* of well-being. Consider the following four judgments.

1. Other things being equal, well-being is undermined when someone hooks up to the experience machine (a device that is supposed to produce realistic experiences by feeding electrical impulses into one's brain).
2. Other things being equal, well-being is undermined when someone has false friends who seem genuine.
3. Other things being equal, well-being is not promoted when someone's desire to count the blades of grass on the college lawn (with no further purpose) is satisfied.

[handwritten margin note: Tension Because philosophers Can't really tell us what is good or Bad for it?]

4. Other things being equal, well-being is undermined when someone has a longer commute (e.g., has a larger house in the suburbs rather than a smaller house in the city, nearer one's place of work) (Stutzer and Frey 2008).

Many philosophers have rejected theories of well-being that do not accord with the first three judgments. So in practice, the traditional approach is committed to the proposition that the first three judgments are about the *nature* of well-being and so constitute evidence that a theory of well-being must account for. (That's not to say that every philosopher thinks these judgments are true, e.g., Crisp 2006, Mendola 2006.) But the fourth judgment is different. Even if it is true, and even if we have overwhelming evidence that it is true, it is not a judgment about the *nature* of well-being. It is an empirical judgment about what tends to foster or undermine well-being. Proponents of the traditional approach can admit that this empirical judgment is one about which philosophers have "no special expertise."[1]

1. It is natural to suppose that the traditional approach makes a distinction about the way we come to know about the nature of well-being and the way we come to know about the causes, effects, and correlates of well-being. On anyone's view, knowledge about the causes, effects, and correlates of well-being is a posteriori—we know these things only by experience. It is natural to suppose that the traditional approach assumes that knowledge about the nature of well-being is a priori—the nature of well-being is knowable independent of experience. We cannot know simply by reflection, without doing a scientific study, that longer commutes undermine well-being; but we can know simply by reflection, without doing a scientific study, that hooking up to the experience machine undermines well-being. This would explain why philosophers can have expertise about the nature of well-being without having expertise about the causes, effects, and correlates of well-being. The view that science is a posteriori while philosophy is a priori surely grounds some philosophers' views about how to properly study well-being. But others might reasonably deny that they are committed to this hard-and-fast distinction. So for the purposes of casting as wide a net as possible, I will not assume that this thesis is part of the traditional approach.

2.2. Philosophy First

The distinction between judgments about the nature of well-being and judgments about the causes and correlates of well-being leads ineluctably to a Philosophy First approach. The intuitive idea is that the philosophical project of accounting for the nature of well-being is foundational and logically prior to the empirical project of identifying the causes, effects, and correlates of well-being. More specifically, the Philosophy First approach relies on the following two ideas:

a. *Insulation*: Philosophy is insulated from psychology. The primary evidence for or against a theory about the nature of well-being comes from our judgments about the nature of well-being. Empirical findings about the causes, effects, or correlates of well-being are not relevant evidence for or against a theory about the nature of well-being.

b. *Vulnerability*: Psychology is vulnerable to philosophy. Any empirical claim about well-being must make substantive assumptions about the nature of well-being that are ultimately validated or invalidated by the correct philosophical theory about the nature of well-being.

When it comes to the study of well-being, the philosophical project is foundational in the sense that psychology cannot safely ignore philosophy but philosophy can safely ignore psychology.

We can appreciate the power of the Philosophy First approach with an example. Studies suggest that meditation tends to foster well-being (Shapiro, Schwartz, and Santerre 2002). But all any such study can show is that meditation tends to foster X, where X is an empirical property that is thought to accurately measure well-being. We can distinguish two claims:

1. Meditation tends to foster X.
2. Meditation tends to foster well-being.

(1) is the sort of claim about which philosophers have no special expertise. Suppose it's true. Whether (2) follows from (1) depends on whether psychologists are right that X is a good measure or proxy for well-being. But this will largely depend on what well-being is; and this is, on the traditional approach, something we can discover only by philosophical reflection on our commonsense judgments about the nature of well-being. An accurate account of the nature of well-being will be delivered by the correct *philosophical* theory of well-being. The argument for the Philosophy First approach takes the form of a dilemma. The assumption that X is a good measure of well-being is either consistent with the correct philosophical theory of well-being or it's not. If it is consistent, then (2) might be true but it can't undermine the philosophical theory. If it is not consistent with the correct philosophical theory of well-being, then it's (2), the *empirical* claim about meditation, that is in jeopardy. Suppose that the psychologists who performed the study presupposed a mistaken view about the nature of well-being: They found that meditation tends to bring about states of pleasure of the sort the hedonist would identify with well-being, but hedonism (we are supposing) is false. In this situation, we would conclude that even though the study has shown *something*—namely, that meditation tends to bring about pleasure—it hasn't necessarily shown that meditation tends to foster *well-being*. (For an argument along these lines, see Tiberius 2004.) And so the philosophical theory of well-being is invulnerable to psychological findings (Insulation) and psychological findings purporting to be about well-being are vulnerable to philosophical theorizing (Vulnerability).

2.3. A Challenge to the Traditional Approach

The traditional approach has all the benefits of incumbency. Philosophers understand and are comfortable with it. But it requires a robust faith in the accuracy of our commonsense judgments about well-being. It assumes that our pre-scientific convictions are so worthy of belief that it is appropriate that they form the primary evidential base for a theory about the nature of well-being. Proponents of the traditional approach might offer a number of arguments for this bracing optimism. Perhaps we employ a faculty of rational reflection that puts us in a position to know the essence or nature of well-being. Or perhaps we are actually investigating what we mean by the expression "well-being," and since the expression means the same thing in both true and false sentences, it doesn't matter to the accuracy of our study whether it appears in true or false sentences. Or perhaps we are trying to capture the content of the *concept* of well-being, where we can suss that content even if it is sometimes embedded in false beliefs. Each of these possibilities raises further worries. If we are using some faculty of rational reflection, what is this faculty? And why should we think that it is *so* reliable that its judgments should make up the primary evidence for a theory of well-being? And if we are investigating the meaning of "well-being" or the concept of well-being, why should we think that this meaning or concept accurately reflects the true nature of well-being? There may be good answers to these questions. And we could explore these various rabbit holes for a long time. My goal here, though, is not to argue that the traditional approach relies on false assumptions. My goal is to argue that its bold optimism about common sense raises enough doubts to make it reasonable to adopt an alternative approach to investigating the nature of well-being.

(margin note:) we are making well-being into what we want it to be

(margin note:) Theses

The epistemic immodesty of the traditional approach can be put in sharp relief if we consider the diverse range of everyday judgments people have about well-being. Recent studies suggest that people in different cultures and socioeconomic groups diverge, sometimes dramatically, in some of their philosophically significant judgments (Knobe and Nichols 2008, 2013). But we don't need to conduct an experiment to find such diversity. There is a robust diversity in the commonsense judgments of Western philosophers who are experts on well-being. Here are three examples.

The Experience Machine. Consider two people who have exactly the same experiences, but one is genuinely engaged with the world and the other is prone in a laboratory with a machine feeding electrical impulses into her brain (Nozick 1974). Do the two people with exactly the same experiences have the same degree of well-being? Most philosophers think they don't (Nozick 1974) while others, including many hedonists, think they do (Crisp 2006).

Remote Desires. We have desires that extend in time and space far beyond our ken. Examples of remote desires include the desire for posthumous fame, the desire for a stranger to flourish, the desire for some distant future scenario (functional jet packs by the twenty-fourth century), or some quirky desire we could never know is satisfied (a prime number of atoms in the universe) (Parfit 1984, Griffin 1986, Kagan 1998). Does satisfaction of these remote desires promote our well-being? Insofar as these remote desires do not impinge upon our experience, hedonists think they do not. Among desire theorists, who hold (very roughly) that a person's well-being involves her getting what she wants, there is a range of opinion. Mark Lukas argues that satisfaction of every actual desire, including remote desires, promotes well-being, although he seems to readily admit that this requires that one "embrace the absurdity and simply deny the intuition that some desires are irrelevant to well-being" (2010, 21). Mark Overvold suggests that the only desires whose satisfaction promotes a person's well-being are those whose satisfaction logically requires her existence; and so the satisfaction of remote desires does not promote well-being (1982). Other philosophers, however, contend that satisfaction or frustration of posthumous desires can affect a person's well-being (Brandt 1979, Kavka 1986, Portmore 2007). James Griffin distinguishes between informed satisfied desires that can and cannot count toward a person's well-being as follows: "What counts for me, therefore, is what enters my life with no doing from me, what I bring into my life, and what I do with my life" (1986, 22). I interpret this to mean that as long as a remote informed desire is properly connected to one's life plan, its satisfaction promotes the person's well-being. Griffin's restriction rules out some remote desires (e.g., the jet pack or prime number of atoms desires) but not all of them (e.g., the desire for posthumous fame).

The Thriving Wicked. Josef is a wicked man who enjoys inflicting pain on others. He lives in a wicked culture where inflicting pain on a religious minority is endorsed and rewarded. Josef lives a long life, doing work that he enjoys and finds satisfying and for which he is richly rewarded. In most every way, Josef lives a life of comfort, pleasure, and success. Despite his positive experiences and getting most of what he wants, despite his positive evaluations of his life, Josef certainly does not deserve a high degree of well-being. But does he nonetheless have a high degree of well-being? Once again, philosophers do not speak with one voice on this issue. Many philosophers think it is obvious, though unfortunate, that the wicked can have well-being. Other philosophers disagree. For any theory, such as Aristotle's, that makes virtuous activity, or even minimal moral decency, essential to well-being, Josef cannot have well-being (Kraut 1979, Swanton 2003, Hursthouse 2013).

For the traditional approach, each of these cases is meant to elicit a commonsense judgment that is supposed to form part of the evidential base for a theory of well-being. But philosophers have different commonsense judgments about these cases. How are such disagreements to be resolved? This is a tricky predicament because philosophers are adept at building theories that fit their judgments. Philosophers begin with their own commonsense judgments. And they proceed to build an assortment of clever, interesting, and sometimes beautiful theories on their idiosyncratic evidential foundations. But without some principled way to decide which evidential foundation is the right one, the traditional approach runs the risk of congealing into a sterile stalemate. Given the current state of the debate, one can be forgiven for thinking this is something more than a risk.

It is impossible to articulate a consistent theory that accounts for the intuitions of every philosopher—even if we restrict ourselves only to those philosophers who are experts on well-being. So if we are committed to the traditional approach, we need to make some decisions. Whose intuitions should my theory be trying to account for? Perhaps my own. But this assumes that my judgments are more accurate than those of highly accomplished philosophers whom I respect and admire. And regardless of how much confidence I might have in my own judgments, that seems like a risky proposition. But if my goal is to capture someone else's commonsense judgments, then I am at a loss. *Whose?*

And why *theirs*? The diversity challenge brings to life the epistemological problem for the traditional approach. But the epistemological problem is fundamental. Even if the diversity problem
disappeared, even if everyone suddenly found themselves with
perfectly consistent intuitions that support (say) hedonism, the
epistemological problem would still be pressing: On what
grounds are we justified in believing those well-being judgments
are *all* true rather than just *mostly* true? The inclusive approach
has the resources to resolve this problem.

2.4. The Inclusive Approach to the Rescue

By flooding the evidential base with scientific findings, the inclusive approach provides a robust fund of evidence that might
favor certain commonsense judgments over others. If the theory
that best accounts for the entirety of the scientific and commonsense evidence implies that the hedonist is wrong about the experience machine, this would give us principled grounds to
reject the hedonist's judgment. Of course, there is no guarantee
that the inclusive approach can resolve every piece of disputed
evidence. But philosophical methods seldom come with guarantees. In the face of the never-ending deadlock bequeathed to us
by the traditional approach, why not see how far the inclusive
approach can take us?

Before putting the inclusive approach into practice, I have a
confession. The theory that drops out of the inclusive approach
does not always accord with my own commonsense judgments
about well-being. But since I reject the traditional approach and
its unbending faith in the quality of our considered, everyday
opinions, this is not a deal-breaker. I embrace a somewhat counterintuitive theory because it fits so well with such a large body
of evidence, including *most* of my considered judgments about
well-being. The vast majority of readers should expect the same.

[handwritten margin notes: "Even though this approach sometimes goes against his own judgement he's willing to take the risk in it"; "it fits his Theory of well being"]

The theory proposed here will fail to accord perfectly with your commonsense judgments. This should not be, by itself, a reason to doubt the theory. Given the diversity of commonsense judgments about well-being, every consistent theory will violate some people's judgments. In the end, some of us—perhaps most or even all of us—will have to relinquish some of our firmly held intuitions about well-being. Many of us might find this painful or uncomfortable. But there is no better end for an everyday opinion than to die in the service of a theory that best accounts for all the available evidence.

3. The Solomonic Strategy

Some philosophers will respond to the diversity of common sense by adopting the Solomonic strategy: Take "well-being" to be systematically ambiguous and define different senses of it to accord with various conceptions of well-being. There is no limit to how many different senses of "well-being" we can parcel out— one to hedonism (so that the experience machine makes no difference to well-being$_1$), another to desire theories (so that the satisfaction of posthumous desires makes a difference to well-being$_2$), yet another to Aristotle (so that the non-virtuous cannot have well-being$_3$), and so on. We can define a sense of "well-being" that captures even the quirkiest commonsense judgments. The Solomonic strategy is very flexible, which is its strength and its fatal flaw. It is attractive insofar as it promises to resolve the well-being debate while partially validating the claims of all contenders. But it trades philosophical and psychological theorizing about the nature of well-being for linguistic description. Describing the ways different speakers use the expression "well-being" is an interesting empirical question. But it is not my question. I want to know what well-being *is*.

All of these strategies still he and doesn't know what well-Being IS

(margin handwriting: "not just one strategy", "A set of diff ideas & categories", "Sets up the Bigger picture of what well-be...")

Despite its inadequacy as a starting point of inquiry, something like the Solomonic strategy might end up winning the day. Suppose that what best organizes and explains the entirety of the evidence is not a single master category, but a set of different categories. This sort of fragmentation is not uncommon. For example, natural selection is the central process for explaining the history of life on Earth. But it is not the only one. Genetic drift and sexual selection are also important mechanisms. Philosophers often cite jade as an example of a fragmented category. What we know as jade is actually two different kinds of mineral, nephrite and jadeite. In recent years, philosophers have argued that categories central to psychology are fragmented. Paul Griffiths has argued that emotion is not unified enough to be understood to be a single psychological category. Emotion is best understood to be a number of quite different categories with different provenances and causal profiles (1997). Edouard Machery has argued that the psychological category *concept* is similarly fragmented (2009). None of these cases for fragmentation are based on the idea that people use a word (like "jade," "emotion," or "concept") in different ways. The right way to argue for fragmentation is that taking some category to be fragmented best organizes and explains the evidence. It might be that well-being is a fragmented category. I don't think it is. But future developments could prove me wrong.

(margin handwriting: "I think it is")

4. Conclusion

Any method or approach must ultimately be judged by the quality of its product. The product of the traditional approach to the study of well-being has been rampant theoretical dissensus. Peruse the philosophical literature on well-being and you will find a diverse smorgasbord of theories from which you can select the one that best fits your commonsense judgments. Profound disagreement is not a temporary aberration that will resolve itself with more time and study. It is the entirely predictable result of an approach to philosophy that tells us to build theories that capture our commonsense judgments despite the fact that we have no consensus about those judgments. Even so, the traditional approach dominates the philosophical landscape. It has not had enough success to deserve the hegemony it currently enjoys.

I have proposed an alternative approach to the study of well-being. It is inclusive because it takes the study of well-being to be a joint venture, one that requires both the philosopher's theories and the scientist's facts. By the end of this book, I hope to convince you of the power and the promise of the inclusive approach. But I have not argued that the traditional approach is based on false assumptions or that it is doomed to fail. Nor have I argued that the inclusive approach is sure to succeed. My claim is that the traditional approach is not so clearly superior to the inclusive approach that it deserves the supremacy it currently enjoys. Every method makes risky assumptions. No matter how obvious or inevitable some approach might appear to us, there is always a chance that it will lead to a dead end. So why put all our methodological eggs in one basket? As a discipline, we improve our chances of developing a powerful theory if we resist methodological uniformity and adopt a range of different, clear, bold plans for studying well-being (Kitcher 1990). For now, I am content to argue that the inclusive approach deserves a chance.

I should mention that while the inclusive approach is unorthodox in the study of well-being, elements of it can be found in the work of recent philosophers (e.g., Tiberius 2006, 2014; Haybron 2011a; Alexandrova 2012). What's more, the approach is familiar in other areas of philosophy. For example, longstanding debates about the existence and nature of belief, emotions, and consciousness take as evidence both common sense lore and scientific findings (e.g., Stich 1983, Griffiths 1997, Block 2005). In *Knowledge and Its Place in Nature* (2002), Hilary Kornblith employs something very much like the inclusive approach to articulate and defend a reliabilist theory of knowledge. Kornblith's example is an important precedent since he applied the approach to the study of a category taken to be central to a normative branch of philosophy.

A critic might argue that the inclusive approach does not rest on firmer evidential foundations than the traditional approach, since it trades the potentially confused intuitions of philosophers for the potentially confused intuitions of philosophers, psychologists, and laypeople. But this is not an accurate description of the inclusive approach. The scientific evidence does not simply reflect a group of people's commonsense judgments. We can't recreate the scientific evidence by asking psychologists what they think about the nature of well-being. The inclusive approach assumes that the explosion of scientific research on well-being over the past two decades has taught us something about *well-being*, a real state of the world. The inclusive approach recommends that we consider these findings in trying to provide an account of the nature of well-being. If psychology has learned nothing about well-being over the past few decades, then the inclusive approach will fail. But no approach comes without risk. In fact, given the failure of the traditional approach to home in on a preferred theory or a family of theories, I would suggest that the inclusive approach introduces no more risk than philosophers have gladly borne for millennia.

[handwritten margin note: main point]

Chapter 3

Positive Causal Networks and the Network Theory of Well-Being

Positive Psychology has no agreed upon definition. My thesis in this chapter and the next is that Positive Psychology is the study of the structure and dynamics of positive causal networks (PCNs). PCNs are underappreciated denizens of our scientific worldview. The case for my thesis is an exercise in pure philosophy of science. It implies nothing about well-being. So while I could have written these chapters without mentioning well-being, I haven't. One of my goals in this book is to defend the network theory of well-being, the view that a person's level of well-being is a function of the strength of her PCN and PCN fragments. Since this chapter explains what PCNs and PCN fragments are, it makes sense, for expository purposes, to occasionally pause to explain the network theory. But even if you don't buy the idea that PCNs have anything to do with well-being, I still hope to convince you that they are Positive Psychology's primary object of study.

Scientific Evidence (handwritten margin note)

1. Positive Causal Networks in Psychology

Psychologists have identified many instances of positive causal networks. For example, in a wide-ranging review article, Lyubomirsky, King, and Diener make a clear case for the existence of PCNs. They argue that Positive Psychology has discovered a set of relatively stable happiness–success feedback loops.

Success leads to happiness vs. *Happiness leads to success* (handwritten margin notes)

> [H]appy people are successful and flourishing people. Part of the explanation for this phenomenon undoubtedly comes from the fact that success leads to happiness. Our review, however, focuses on the reverse causal direction—that happiness, in turn, leads to success . . . [T]he evidence seems to support our conceptual model that happiness causes many of the successful outcomes with which it correlates. Furthermore, the data suggest that the success of happy people may be mediated by the effects of positive affect and the characteristics that it promotes. It appears that happiness, rooted in personality and in past successes, leads to approach behaviors that often lead to further success (2005, 845–846).

Lyubomirsky, King, and Diener are proposing a schema for an important class of positive causal networks. They spell out many ways in which the top arrow (Happiness → Success) can come about (Figure 3.1). Of course, successful people can be unhappy, and so the opposite arrow is not automatic. Psychologists sometimes call PCNs that have this cyclical structure "upward spirals" (e.g., Loewenstein 1994). These upward spirals help explain the relative stability of PCNs.

The most sustained case for the existence and importance of PCNs is Barbara Fredrickson's articulation and defense of the

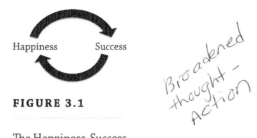

FIGURE 3.1

The Happiness-Success
Cycle

Broaden and Build Hypothesis. Positive moods and emotions tend to broaden a person's "thought-action repertoire, widening the array of the thoughts and actions that come to mind" (2001, 220). As a result of this broadened thought-action repertoire, the person is more effectively able to build durable physical, social, intellectual, and psychological resources "that can be drawn on later in other contexts and in other emotional states" (1998, 307). These resources are durable in the sense that they last much longer than the emotion. Fredrickson's Broaden and Build Hypothesis proposes the following multiply realizable positive causal chain:

Positive affect → Broadened thought-action repertoires → Increased resources.

Add to this the plausible speculation that having greater social, psychological, material, and intellectual resources tends to promote success in ways that foster positive affect. Now what we have is a general schema of an important class of positive causal cycles (Figure 3.2). Figures 3.1 and 3.2 are not in competition. A successful relationship might be an example of both the happiness-success cycle and also the broaden-and-build cycle.

Fredrickson argues that the Broaden and Build Hypothesis shows how the positive emotions might have been evolutionary

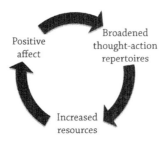

FIGURE 3.2

Fredrickson's Broaden and
Build Cycle

adaptations. It is widely accepted that our (intuitively) negative
emotions, emotions that narrow our thought-action repertoires,
are adaptations. Consider the characteristic cascade of psychological and physiological changes associated with fear. They involve the fast and automatic focusing of our attention, our
thoughts, and our behavioral dispositions in ways that help us
avoid or escape dangerous situations. This would have been advantageous to our ancestors, helping them to survive and repro-
duce. A similar case can be made for anger and disgust being
evolutionary adaptations. But what about the "basic" positive
emotions? Fredrickson speculates:

> Human ancestors who succumbed to the urges sparked by
> positive emotions to play, explore, and so on would have by
> consequence accrued more personal resources. When these
> same ancestors later faced inevitable threats to life and
> limb, their greater personal resources would have translated
> into greater odds of survival, and, in turn, greater odds of
> living long enough to reproduce. To the extent, then, that
> the capacity to experience positive emotions is genetically

encoded, this capacity, through the process of natural selection, would have become part of universal human nature
(2001, 220).

The case for PCNs as a basic unit of study in the empirical literature on well-being does not depend on the details of this adapta-
tionist account of the positive emotions. But it offers a suggestive evolutionary explanation for the psychological bases of
PCNs: Among our ancestors, those that had the genetically en-
dowed capacity to become readily enmeshed in PCNs may have
had a selective advantage.

2. What Are Positive Causal Networks? (WHAT)

So what are positive causal networks? There is a natural tempta-
tion for philosophers to try to answer this question with a classical account of PCNs: an account framed in terms of singly necessary and jointly sufficient conditions; an account that uses
only clear and precise terms; and an account that captures our
commonsense, intuitive understanding of PCNs. Although I
would be glad to have a classical account of PCNs, insisting on
one at this stage of our investigation is a mistake. Our target is
a *scientific* concept, not a commonsense one. While we must
begin with our commonsense ideas in trying to make sense of
PCNs—Where else would we begin?—the ultimate goal is not to
capture our commonsense ideas but to improve them. Relatively
young scientific posits are seldom neatly and accurately characterized. Even when science delivers a classical account of a posit
like water or lightning, it is developed only after considerable
empirical investigation. Competent investigations into the
nature of scientific categories do not typically begin with great

conceptual lucidity. And so we should not expect greater clarity than the subject matter currently affords.

Instead of a classical account, I will propose a modest empirical account of PCNs. A modest account allows us to reliably identify PCNs and distinguish them from other things in the world. It is explicitly provisional. As we learn more about PCNs, the hope is that we will be able to develop something more stylish. According to the provisional modest account, PCNs can be identified and distinguished from other scientific posits in terms of three characteristic features.

1. PCNs are made up of an agent's feelings, emotions, attitudes, behaviors, traits, and accomplishments.
2. PCNs are homeostatic property clusters: A family of properties that tend to co-occur because "[e]ither the presence of some of the properties . . . tends to favor the presence of the others, or there are underlying mechanisms or processes which tend to maintain the presence of the" property cluster (Boyd 1989, 16). As with many homeostatic property clusters, positive causal networks will have "borderline" cases in which there is no fact of the matter about whether something is or is not a positive causal network, and they might lack an essence, a property or mechanism that occurs in all instances of the cluster (Boyd 1989, 16–17).

Psychologists have identified many homeostatically clustered sets of feelings, emotions, attitudes, behaviors, traits, and accomplishments. Their cyclical patterns suggest that "the presence of some of the properties . . . tends to favor the presence of the others" in the cluster (Boyd 1989, 16).

The characterization of PCNs as a homeostatically clustered set of feelings, emotions, attitudes, behaviors, traits, and accomplishments is incomplete. There are negative or vicious causal networks. People who are depressed suffer from negative feelings, attitudes, behaviors, and dysfunctions, and these can causally build upon and reinforce one another. There may be neutral networks, neither positive nor negative. Consider the unambitious, worn-down bureaucrat marking time in a marginally satisfying job. We can see how such a person's flat affect and lack of energy might contribute to his dull life and vice versa. The third characteristic feature of PCNs marks off what makes a causal network positive rather than negative or neutral.

3. A homeostatically clustered network of feelings, emotions, attitudes, behaviors, traits, and accomplishments is positive (rather than negative or neutral) if it consists of relatively more of the following sorts of states:
   a. psychological states that feel good—that have a positive hedonic tone;
   b. states (psychological or not) that when present in this network tend to bring about psychological states that have a positive hedonic tone;
   c. states that the agent values;
   d. states that the agent's culture values.

The first two conditions describe causal networks as homeostatic clusters of emotions, attitudes, traits, and accomplishments. The third condition distinguishes one kind of causal network from others. It says only that among all the causal networks (i.e., homeostatic clusters of emotions, attitudes, traits, and accomplishments) in the world, the positive ones are those with a high concentration of states that feel good, that bring about states that feel good, and that are valued by the person or her culture. The appeal to what a person or culture "values" is meant to be descriptive. It can be measured in terms of what a person is disposed to endorse, praise, pursue, or explicitly say she values. The appeal to experiences with "positive hedonic tone" is trickier but is also meant to be descriptive.

Given our current state of knowledge, I don't think we are in a position to offer an informative account of what it is for a psychological state to have a "positive hedonic tone." If someone were to propose a promising reductive, neurochemical account of such positive experiences, the resulting philosophical hullabaloo would be exciting. But until that day comes, if it comes, the best we can do is repeat the wisdom of Louis Armstrong, who, when pressed to define jazz, said, "Man, if you gotta ask, you'll never know." We can, of course, point to stereotypical examples of experiences with positive hedonic tone, such as the physical pleasures (e.g., sexual, gastronomic), the feelings involved with positive social interactions (love, close friendship) and aesthetic experiences (e.g., listening to a symphony, looking at great art). These standard examples usually involve a kind of surplus pleasure—a localized internal feeling or sensation that goes beyond one's experience of external events. Not all positively valenced experiences involve this kind of surplus pleasure. A person totally engrossed in an engaging activity might not feel anything like the surplus pleasure involved in tasting a crisp, juicy apple. She might only feel deep engagement with the details of the specific task at hand (Csikszentmihalyi 2008). And when her project is a particularly large one, she might go long stretches of time, even years, without the "surplus" feeling of satisfaction that accompanies overcoming a difficult challenge. It is only a slight exaggeration to say that we can become addicted to activities that involve this kind of experience, as anyone who has gotten hooked on doing crossword puzzles or studying chess openings can attest. This feeling of being thoroughly engrossed is positively valenced and, arguably, has a positive hedonic tone. I say "arguably" because it appears that what I am claiming are two elements of pleasurable experiences, the surplus pleasure and the desire or commitment to pursue an activity, are subserved by different neurological mechanisms (Kringelbach and Berridge 2010, 2012). It might be better to draw a firm distinction between these two kinds of experience, even though they normally co-occur. A scary feature of the inclusive approach is that future scientific findings can disconfirm a philosophical theory. On the flip side, the inclusive approach also allows a philosopher to reserve the right to amend a theory in the light of future evidence. So for now, I will combine all these experiences under the heading of states with "positive hedonic tone" even though I suspect that this will need revision.

The best way to understand condition (3) is as an empirical speculation about the *dynamics* of causal networks. Causal networks, by definition, have inertia. Once a homeostatic cluster of properties is in place, it will tend to be self-perpetuating. Let's say that a network's *causal drivers* are those states that are part of the network that tend to establish, maintain, or strengthen the network. (For a more careful and detailed account of the dynamics of PCNs, see chapter 4.) The empirical speculation grounding condition (3) is that causal drivers of PCNs tend to be states that are valued and that involve positive experience. That's not to say that every state that feels good or is valued is a causal driver of a PCN. But when you find a causal driver of a PCN, it will usually be a state that feels good or that is valued by the agent or her culture. Among the plausible causal drivers of Felicity's PCN are her athletic and academic success, her joie de vivre, her friendliness, and her courage. One explanation for why these states are causal drivers of Felicity's PCN is that Felicity and her culture value them. Other plausible causal drivers of Felicity's PCN include her good

moods and the feelings of love and camaraderie she shares
with her family and friends. These states both have a positive
hedonic tone and are endorsed by Felicity and her culture.
Once again, the positive experience and pro-attitudes explain
why these states are causal drivers of Felicity's PCN, why they
tend to bring about further states that comprise her PCN.
The causal drivers of PCNs tend to clump together. This co-
occurrence is not an accident.

This picture of the causal drivers of PCNs is surely too crude.
Further investigation into the dynamics of PCNs will give us a
sharper understanding of their causal drivers. But condition (3)
is fine as a first, rough approximation. Recall that what I prom-
ised you was a modest account of PCNs. And the account on offer
is certainly that. Despite its plainness, it does the job. It allows
us to identify positive causal networks.

3. Positive Causal Networks and Well-Being

The natural instinct of many philosophers will be to attack
condition (3) with counterexamples showing that a person's
well-being is *not* improved every time she is in a state that has
one or more of the features (a)–(d). Suppose David is a member
of a political party or a religious denomination that is highly
regarded in his culture. That fact, by itself, might not promote his well-being. But doesn't the network theory imply
that it must promote his well-being, given that part of what
makes a causal network positive is that it consists of states
valued by a person's culture? No. To see this, let's distinguish
two questions:

   a. What makes a PCN stronger or weaker?
   b. What makes a causal network positive?

Condition (3) only answers the second question. It provides an identifying mark of positive causal networks. But condition (3) does not imply anything about how strong a PCN is. Just because David is a member of a political party or religious denomination that is highly regarded in his culture, the network theory does not imply that the membership necessarily strengthens his well-being. David's membership might not be a causal driver of his PCN. In fact, his membership might cause David such shame that it destroys his PCN, and so, according to the network theory, his well-being. Let's turn to the question of what does strengthen or weaken PCNs.

4. The Strength of PCNs

A change to a person's positive causal network strengthens that network if it makes it more robust—the network is better able to persist in a wider range of plausible environments. A change weakens a person's PCN if it makes the network less robust—the network is less able to persist in a wide range of plausible environments. Psychological instruments exist that are reasonable measures of robustness.[1] But my plan here is to stick to the intuitive idea of robustness. PCNs are homeostatic systems, like living organisms or running engines. Changes strengthen the system when they make the system tougher, sturdier, more durable, harder to extinguish. Changes weaken the system when they make it more delicate, less durable, easier to extinguish. My speculation is that there are two ways to strengthen or weaken a person's PCN: (i) by changing the intensity of the states that compose the network or (ii) by

1. For example, resiliency (Werner 1983, Benard 1991), hardiness (Kobasa 1979), and grit (Duckworth et al. 2007) are constructs meant to capture the ability of people to thrive in adverse or challenging circumstances.

changing the size of the network (i.e., by increasing or decreasing the number of states that comprise it). Let's consider each of these in turn.

Suppose the relationship between the degree of Felicity's academic success and the strength of her PCN is monotonic—any increase in success brings an increase in robustness (Figure 3.3). Given the shape of this robustness curve, Felicity's well-being is at its peak when she is maximally successful in her schoolwork. This is the *robustness maximum* for academic success: the degree of academic success that most effectively contributes to the promotion of Felicity's PCN.

I want to make three general points. First, the robustness charts are illustrative examples. Their axes represent relative increases or decreases in the relevant states. Second, robustness curves are to be interpreted *causally*: In Felicity's plausible environments, an increase in academic success will causally contribute to the robustness of Felicity's PCN. So moving up the robustness scale implies that, all else being equal, Felicity's PCN will be able to persist in a wider range of plausible environments. Of course, in many circumstances, it will be useful or perhaps even

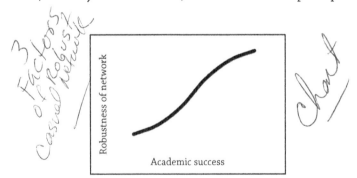

FIGURE 3.3

Robustness Curve for Academic Success

necessary to interpret robustness curves in probabilistic terms. But for theoretical purposes, the network theory takes robustness curves to represent the *actual contribution* a factor (such as academic success or positive affect) makes to the robustness of a positive causal network. And third, robustness curves are indexed to a person and her plausible environments (i.e., environments the individual might realistically find herself in). A change in the plausible environments (where other personality factors count as part of the environment) might well change the shape of a robustness curve. So for a different person or for the same person in a different context, the robustness curve for academic success might have a different shape.

Let's consider the relationship between Felicity's curiosity and the strength of her PCN (Figure 3.4). The robustness maximum for curiosity is somewhere between the extremes. A middling degree of curiosity most effectively contributes to the robustness of Felicity's positive causal networks (to their capacity to persist in a wider range of plausible environments). And so at this degree of curiosity, Felicity's well-being is at its peak, all other things being equal.

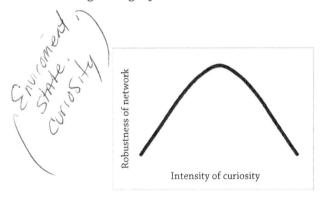

FIGURE 3.4

Robustness Curve for Curiosity

A concave robustness curve for a personality characteristic provides a way to spell out something akin to Aristotle's idea of the virtues as "golden means" between extremes of deficiency and excess (for example, the virtue of bravery as the golden mean between the deficiencies of cowardice and foolhardiness). There is evidence that some traits have concave robustness profiles. They have an intensity "sweet spot"—a moderately high level, neither too intense nor too faint—that is most effective at maintaining a person's PCN over the long term. For example, the high levels of positive affect associated with mania undermine PCNs; while positive moods improve our creativity they appear to inhibit logical thinking (Melton 1995); among young men, high positive affect can lead to high-risk behavior that can lead to harmful results that undermine PCNs (Friedman 1993, Martin et al. 2002); while the highest levels of happiness in an adult population are most strongly correlated with close relationships and volunteer work, slightly lower but still above average levels of happiness are most strongly correlated with income, education, and political participation (Oishi, Diener, and Lucas 2007). On the other hand, Peterson and Seligman suggest, perhaps contrary to common sense, that the robustness curve for self-control is not concave but monotonic. Greater self-control tends to lead to more robust PCNs (2004, 508). So here is the first condition on the graded nature of PCNs.

Intensity: Other things being equal, a PCN is stronger insofar as the intensities of the states that constitute the network are closer to their robustness maxima.

In Felicity's situation, her PCN is strengthened with any improvement to her academic success or any change to her curiosity level that moves it closer to its "golden mean" (its robustness maximum).

It is worth making two points here. First, the existence of concave robustness curves shows that condition (3) in the modest account of PCNs is an identifying mark of a causal network that is positive, not an account of what makes such a network stronger or more positive. If a state with a positive hedonic tone is a link in a PCN, increasing the hedonic intensity of that state does not necessarily strengthen the PCN. Whether it strengthens the PCN (and so, according to the network theory, promotes well-being) depends on the effect of that increased intensity on the robustness of the PCN. Second, framing robustness in atomistic terms—in terms of the robustness curve of a single link in the network, such as academic success or curiosity—is far too simple. Robustness curves for many traits are context-sensitive. Peterson and Seligman note that depending on contextual and personality factors, curiosity can promote activity that contributes to well-being or activity that does not (2004, 135–136). Persistence backfires if one is pursuing unachievable goals or using ineffective methods (239). In environments where one might face genuine risks and dangers, hope and optimism can undermine well-being by engendering a lack of caution—for example, when young people engage in risky behavior or don't take appropriate precautionary measures. What's more, optimism among older folks "predicts depression in the wake of stressful events. Perhaps extreme optimism among the elderly is unrealistic, and the occurrence of something terrible can devastate the optimistic older individual" (577). A change in the intensity of one link of a network can change the intensity of other links in the network. (It is, after all, a network.) And this can considerably complicate matters given that some robustness curves are context-sensitive: A change in the intensity of one link can change both the intensity and the robustness curves of other links. The interaction effects can get messy and complicated. So while robustness is

probably best understood as a global feature of positive causal
networks, for the sake of simplicity, I will stick with this atomistic account of robustness.

The second way a person's positive causal networks might be
strengthened or weakened is by increasing or decreasing the
number of states that make up her network. But not just any
states will do. Only adding or subtracting states that are causal
drivers will count as strengthening or weakening the PCN.
Suppose Felicity loses her job and gets a new, less satisfying,
less well-paying job. She therefore loses many of the states
that were associated with her professional success—her high
income, her sense of competence and productivity, her sense of
security, her friendships with her co-workers. Losing these
causal drivers might be so devastating that it completely destroys Felicity's PCN. But it's also possible that she would retain
a modified PCN focused on her relationships, projects, and hobbies. Other things being equal, however, the loss of those causal
drivers makes it easier for unfortunate circumstances to extinguish her PCN altogether. This retrenchment makes Felicity's
PCN less robust, and hence diminishes her well-being. Of
course, Felicity might respond to the loss of these causal drivers
by replacing them with different causal drivers, say, by taking
up a new project. Or she might increase the intensity of her remaining causal drivers, say, by devoting more time and energy
to her friendships. In these ways, Felicity can rebuild the
strength of her PCN.

Consider the relationship between the robustness of Felicity's PCN and the number and variety of causal drivers that
comprise it (Figure 3.5). Without enough causal drivers to establish a network, PCNs cannot get off the ground. Once there
are enough drivers to form an operating network, robustness
increases quickly with size. Then there comes a point of dimin-
ishing marginal returns: Once the network is quite robust,

It can change, it doesn't stay steady

But if numbers power you can manage to substitute

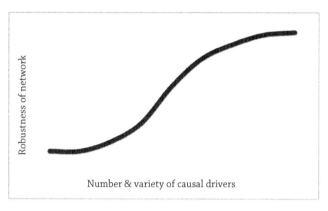

FIGURE 3.5

Robustness and Size

further size increases bring relatively smaller robustness increases. So here is the second condition on the graded nature of PCNs.

> *Size:* Other things being equal, a person's PCN is stronger (weaker) as the number and variety of its causal drivers increase (decrease).

The "other things being equal" hedge is important. If a change in the number and variety of a PCN's causal drivers is accompanied by other changes relevant to robustness, then the impact will be a function of all those interactions.

The well-known Nun Study (Danner, Snowdon, and Friesen 2001) suggests that the variety of positive experiences might be a more important causal driver of PCNs than we might intuitively suppose. Beginning in 1930, nuns who had taken their vows at the School Sisters of Notre Dame religious congregation were asked to "write a short sketch of your life . . . on a single sheet of paper . . . include place of birth, parentage, interesting and edifying events of childhood, schools attended, influences that led to the convent, religious life, and outstanding events" (806). The researchers discovered 180 handwritten autobiographies. An interesting feature of this study is that the participants were very similar. They were all female (obviously), "had the same reproductive and marital histories, had similar social activities and support, did not smoke or drink excessive amounts of alcohol, had virtually the same occupation and socio-economic status, and had comparable access to medical care. Therefore, even though it may be difficult to generalize from this unique population of Catholic sisters, many factors that confound most studies of longevity have been minimized or eliminated" (805–806). The autobiographies were scored for passages that reflected a positive emotional experience (amusement, gratitude, interest), a negative emotional experience (anger, disgust, fear, sadness), or a neutral emotional experience (surprise).

The number of negative emotion sentences in the autobiographies was not correlated with mortality. Nuns who expressed fewer negative emotions did not live longer than nuns who expressed more negative emotions. This result may be a statistical artifact: there were relatively few negative emotion sentences in the autobiographies, less than 5% of all emotion sentences (810–811). But the number of positive emotion sentences in the autobiography was strongly correlated with mortality. Nuns who expressed more positive emotions lived significantly longer than nuns who expressed fewer positive emotions. The difference in median age at death for those in the top quartile and bottom quartile was almost 7 years. The difference in median age of death between the highest and lowest quartile for number of positive emotion *words* was even greater, 9.4 years. But the biggest difference, 10.7 years, was between the highest and lowest quartile in the *variety* of positive emotions (809).

The psychological literature is full of correlations between something that seems trivial (such as a one-page autobiography written in one's 20s) and something very significant (such as life expectancy). Teasing out a detailed explanation for these correlations is sure to be a large task. But the network theory offers a framework for understanding such correlations in terms of self-maintaining positive causal networks. The person who writes an autobiography at 25 that uses a greater number and variety of positive emotion words is more likely to be in a positive causal network. These networks have inertia—they tend to be self-maintaining. And so you're more likely to be in a PCN at 75 if you were in one at 25. Positive causal networks are good for your psychological health. The Nun Study suggests they also contribute to a longer life.

Argument
persuasive
Belief
This is why you'd
Should
Believe

5. PCN Fragments and Well-Being

Many studies in Positive Psychology investigate PCN fragments. A state or set of states is a PCN fragment when it is *or could be* a causal driver in a PCN for that person, keeping relatively constant the sort of person she is (i.e., her personality, her goals, and her general dispositions). Suppose Joy instantiates an extremely robust PCN. Now consider a series of Joys (Joy$_1$, Joy$_2$, etc.) each with a missing link: Each subsequent Joy is missing one more causal driver from Joy's original PCN. Joy$_1$ lacks one link, Joy$_2$ lacks that link and one more, and so on. Eventually, there will be intermediate cases such that there is no fact of the matter about whether that particular Joy is in a PCN. Such borderline cases are to be expected. Then at some further point down the line, Joy (or rather, Joy$_n$) would clearly not instantiate a PCN. But she would still possess PCN fragments—causal drivers that could be part of a positive causal network for Joy.

PCN fragments are important to understanding Positive Psychology because many published studies identify PCN fragments. But they are absolutely crucial to the network theory of well-being. That's because it's possible for a person to be better or worse off even if he is not in a PCN. The presence of PCN *fragments* means a person's life is going better. Even if Gary is not in a PCN, his life might go better being entertained by Harold Lloyd's *Safety Last* than ruminating over his latest misery. Gary enjoying this great silent movie is a PCN fragment. Take all the plausible PCNs Gary *might* be in. Given his temperament, goals, values, and abilities, Gary might find himself in various PCNs involving his profession, his social relationships, and his hobbies. The causal drivers implicated in these networks are all PCN fragments for Gary.

A set of states might be a PCN fragment for one person but not another. Suppose Joe is a misanthrope, unable to enter into any positive causal networks involving friendship. It's not that he can thrive in close friendships but prefers not to; nor is it that he is friendless against his wishes. Rather, Joe is constitutionally incapable of thriving in relationships with other people. In that case, his having a friend, by itself, would not be a PCN fragment. Given Joe's misanthropy, his having a friend would not engender in him the typical feelings of camaraderie, solidarity, and support it would in the rest of us. It would not be a causal driver of his PCN. Joe's friend might, of course, help him to act or feel in ways that are PCN fragments for Joe. And so his friend might make Joe's life better indirectly. But the mere fact that Joe has a friend does not make his life better (see Scanlon 1998a, 116). Consider a less dramatic example. Successfully engaging in an act of mild daredevilry might be a PCN fragment for Daring Dan but not Cautious Charlie.

PCN fragments are by definition not self-maintaining and so it makes no sense to evaluate their strength in terms of their robustness, that is, in terms of their ability to persist in a range of environments. Pat starts playing guitar in a band, but he and his band are neither good nor successful enough for him to be in a PCN centered on his music. He values making music and derives some enjoyment from it, but he keeps at it mostly out of a sense of obligation to his friends. These states—Pat playing music, valuing and enjoying his music— contribute to his well-being because they are PCN fragments. They could be causal drivers in a full-blown PCN for Pat. Given his situation, there are two ways to promote Pat's well-being, to strengthen his PCN fragments. One is by increasing the intensity of the fragment's causal drivers. For example, Pat's well-being increases if his musicianship improves or he begins to derive greater pleasure from playing. Another way to strengthen Pat's PCN fragments is by increasing their size. Pat begins a new relationship or becomes serious about making French pastries, and so his PCN fragments consist of a greater number of potential causal drivers.

A PCN fragment is typically stronger insofar as it consists of causal drivers of greater number or intensity. But there is a significant qualification: A PCN fragment is weakened by any change that makes it more difficult for the person to enter into a PCN. Let's see what happens to Pat's well-being as his positive affect increases (reading the curves from left to right in Figure 3.6). At very low levels of positive affect, increases in positive affect do nothing to aid in the promotion of a PCN (black curve, left). These increases in positive affect do strengthen Pat's PCN fragment (gray curve, left) and so his well-being. Moderate and moderately high levels of positive affect are more likely to kick-start a full-blown PCN (black curve, center). And Pat's well-being strengthens along with his PCN fragments (gray curve, center). But at some point, greater positive affect undermines the promotion of a PCN by causing Pat to engage in risky or

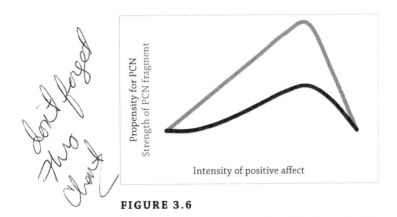

(handwritten marginal note: don't forget this chart)

FIGURE 3.6

Positive Affect and PCN Fragments

imprudent behavior (black curve, right). Once this occurs, once increases in positive affect begin to diminish Pat's ability to have well-being, they begin to diminish his well-being (gray curve, right). Feeling better does not always strengthen PCN fragments. But as long as feeling better does not diminish our chances of getting into a PCN, it improves our well-being.

The intuitive idea is that the way to make your life better is to have more of a good thing (more intense causal drivers) or more good things (greater number of causal drivers) except when they interfere with your ability to have a good life (to enter into a PCN).

6. Conclusion

We happen to live in a world in which there exist homeostatically clustered networks of states that include some combination of feelings, emotions, attitudes, behaviors, traits, and interactions with the world. This sort of network is *positive* if it consists of a high concentration of states that have a positive

(handwritten marginal note: Keywords)

hedonic tone, that tend to bring about other states with a positive hedonic tone, or that the agent or her culture values. The network theory holds that well-being can be understood entirely in terms of PCNs and their fragments. The picture of well-being put forward by the network theory is a graded one. At the lowest rung are people with no well-being at all—they possess no states that might be causal drivers of a positive causal network (i.e., no PCN fragments). Going up the well-being scale, some people possess PCN fragments, but these fragments don't have enough causal drivers to produce a self-maintaining, homeostatic causal network. These people have some degree of well-being, but they are not in a *state* of well-being. At the highest level are people who are in a state of well-being because they instantiate a full-blown PCN. There is no firm boundary between PCN fragments and full-blown PCNs. There are bound to be borderline cases, cases in which there is no fact of the matter about whether the person has enough PCN fragments to actually make up a self-maintaining network. For people in a PCN, they will have greater well-being to the extent that their PCN is more robust—it is better able to persist in a wider range of environments. Typically a person's well-being will be strengthened with any increase to the number, variety, or intensity of the causal drivers making up her PCN. As a general rule, though not invariably, a PCN fragment is stronger insofar as it consists of causal drivers of greater number or intensity.

For those well-versed in theories of well-being, the network theory is somewhat similar to a combined Aristotelian-objective list theory. The part of the theory that appeals to positive causal networks is akin to Aristotle's theory. Both views take well-being to consist of a self-maintaining network of positive traits, emotions, attitudes, experiences, and successful engagement with the world that are non-accidentally connected to each other (Foot 2002, Hursthouse 2002, Kraut

2007). The fundamental difference between the theories is that virtue is essential to well-being for the Aristotelian. (More on this in chapter 5.) The part of the network theory that appeals to PCN fragments is akin to the objective list view (Finnis 1980, Parfit 1984, Griffin 1986, Hurka 1993). Both enumerate a set of states that contribute to a person's well-being. A familiar objection to objective list theories is that they fail to provide a principle for why some states make the "contributes to well-being" list and others don't. The network theory offers a principle of inclusion that allows for personalized lists: States that are potential causal drivers of a person's PCN make the "contributes to well-being" list. So Daring Dan's list of PCN fragments (i.e., factors that would contribute to his well-being) consists of more daring feats than does Cautious Charlie's.

Chapter 4

Positive Causal Networks and Positive Psychology

Just as cytology is the study of cells, Positive Psychology is the study of the structure and dynamics of positive causal networks. Both disciplines are defined and unified by their primary objects of study. Take cells away from cytology and cytology would appear to be a mish-mash without any clear underlying rhyme or reason. Psychologists have not yet explicitly organized Positive Psychology around positive causal networks (PCNs). And so Positive Psychology appears to be a mishmash without any clear underlying rhyme or reason. But this appearance is deceptive. Positive Psychology is a coherent, unified discipline. It's just that its underlying framework has not yet been clearly described.

Before we get started, a warning. Some experts in Positive Psychology might react to this chapter with impatience: "This is *trivial*! You haven't added *anything* to research other people have already done!" In one sense, this reaction would be a sign that the chapter is going well. The correct framework for understanding Positive Psychology *should* seem obvious to those who already understand Positive Psychology. But I would gently suggest that anyone having this reaction is guilty of the hindsight (or "I knew it all along") bias. This is our tendency to take things that are not obvious or predictable to be obvious or predictable after we learn about them. To forestall this reaction, I will open this chapter by reporting how some experts characterize Positive Psychology. It is fair to say that psychologists have not yet hit upon a clear way to characterize this discipline. If we take Positive Psychology to be the study of PCNs, all the ways these experts have characterized Positive Psychology turn out to be true. This is the first piece of evidence for thinking the network theory organizes and makes sense of Positive Psychology (section 1). But to demonstrate the organizing power of PCNs, there is no substitute for slogging through the scientific literature (sections 2–4). Much of Positive Psychology looks for correlations (in survey data) or causal connections (in longitudinal studies or laboratory experiments) among positive feelings, moods, emotions, attitudes, behavioral traits, and objective factors. This research seeks to identify and describe the causal structure of PCNs (section 2). Positive Psychology also seeks to identify factors that establish, maintain, strengthen, or extinguish PCNs. This research investigates the dynamics of PCNs (section 3). Understanding Positive Psychology as the study of PCNs also provides a useful framework for thinking about the well-being of groups (section 4).

1. What Is Positive Psychology?

The crux of the case for the network theory is that it organizes and makes sense of Positive Psychology, the psychological study of well-being. This assumes that Positive Psychology is in need of conceptual regimentation. It is a coherent, unified discipline whose coherence has not yet been clearly articulated. What we have is clutter masking order, not clutter all the way down. Let's start with the clutter.

1.1. Characterizing Positive Psychology

One way to illustrate the conceptual disorder of Positive Psychology is to see how its practitioners define or describe the field. Here are some pithy but vague characterizations.

> Positive Psychology is the scientific study of what goes right in life, from birth to death and at all stops in between (Peterson 2006, 4).

> Positive Psychology aims to help people live and flourish rather than merely to exist (Keyes and Haidt 2003, 3).

> The label of *Positive Psychology* represents those efforts of professionals to help people optimize human functioning by acknowledging strengths as well as deficiencies, and environmental resources in addition to stressors (Wright and Lopez 2005, 42).

Notice that there is no canonical definition of Positive Psychology, no crystalized description that identifies a category in nature that is its object of study. Notice also the use of normative expressions—"what goes right in life," "flourish," "optimize human functioning." The liberal use of philosophically loaded language suggests that these characterizations aim to communicate an intuitive understanding of Positive Psychology. There is nothing wrong with this. But the intuitive gloss should be backed by a clear, accurate account of the field. And that's what's missing.

Rather than being pithy and vague, some characterizations of Positive Psychology have the opposite problem. They are prolix and full of specifics.

The field of Positive Psychology at the subjective level is about valued subjective experiences: well-being, contentment, and satisfaction (in the past); hope and optimism (for the future); and flow and happiness (in the present). At the individual level, it is about positive individual traits: the capacity for love and vocation, courage, interpersonal skill, aesthetic sensibility, perseverance, forgiveness, originality, future mindedness, spirituality, high talent, and wisdom. At the group level, it is about the civic virtues and the institutions that move individuals toward better citizenship: responsibility, nurturance, altruism, civility, moderation, tolerance, and work ethic (Seligman and Csikszentmihalyi 2000, 5).

Anyone who reads this passage will come away with a good understanding of what Positive Psychology is about. But it is a nonexhaustive laundry list of topics investigated by Positive Psychology. It is not a unified description of a coherent scientific discipline.

Characterizations of Positive Psychology are either pithy, vague, and intuitive, or prolix, "listy," and concrete. Despite their differences, each one effectively communicates what Positive Psychology is about. This is unsurprising, as the authors of these definitions are experts in the field. Here is the first test any framework that seeks to understand Positive Psychology must pass: It should explain the sense in which these various characterizations are all true.

1.2. How to Make Sense of Positive Psychology

The inclusive approach holds that a successful theory of well-being should account for or explain the scientific evidence. But how is this supposed to work? My proposal is that the network theory organizes and unifies Positive Psychology by identifying what it studies, namely, positive causal networks. Other scientific disciplines and subdisciplines can be characterized in ways that are pithy and specific.

- Cytology is the study of the structure, composition, and function of cells and their parts.
- Kinematics is a branch of mechanics that studies motion.
- Biochemistry is the study of the chemical substances and processes that occur in living organisms.

These characterizations define a scientific discipline by identifying the categories in nature that are their object of study—cells, motion, chemical substances, living organisms. In the same way, the network theory provides a way to clearly define Positive Psychology by identifying the real category in nature that is its object of study.

Positive causal networks do more than just define a discipline. Without the category *fossil* to unify and organize paleontology, we could not properly understand vertebrate paleontology (the study of fossil vertebrates), paleobotany (the study of fossil plants), or ichnology (the study of fossil tracks and footprints). Without the category fossil, the study of these various objects would not seem to be part of a coherent discipline, but rather a hodgepodge of different subjects. In the same way, without the category positive causal network, Positive Psychology appears shambolic—a wide variety of approaches, each one focusing special attention on its own set of psychological states and measures. Positing the existence of positive causal networks "makes sense" of Positive Psychology by both defining an object of study and by playing a central role in explanations and hypotheses that are important to this discipline.

1.3. Characterizing the Science of Well-Being

Positive Psychology is the study of the structure and dynamics of PCNs. This proposal explains the sense in which all the characterizations of Positive Psychology are true, the vague pithy ones and the wordy catalogs. If Positive Psychology is the study of the structure of PCNs, then it is also the study of "what goes right in life." And if it is the study of the dynamics of PCNs, of how PCNs are established, maintained, and strengthened, it *does* have the capacity to "help people . . . flourish" and "optimize human functioning." This proposal also implies that the prolix characterization of Positive Psychology is accurate insofar as it touches on the three subjective elements of PCNs: positive feelings and emotions (contentment, satisfaction, happiness); positive attitudes (hope, optimism); and positive traits (courage, perseverance, originality, altruism, tolerance, civility). It omits the fourth element of PCNs, successful engagement with the world. But some real-life accomplishments typically accompany any long stretch of the subjective items cited. This is the first line of evidence for the network theory. It is able to interpret the various ways expert practitioners describe Positive Psychology so that all of them turn out to be accurate.

Another way to appreciate the apparent conceptual disarray of Positive Psychology is to note the wide range of approaches different psychologists take to its study. Consider a pair of books that introduce the discipline. A thematically based introduction to the field includes chapters that focus on pleasure, happiness, positive thinking, character strengths, values, interests, wellness, positive relationships, and enabling institutions (Peterson 2006, see also Keyes and Haidt 2003). Each of these topics is an intuitively plausible entry point to the study of well-being. But it is not clear why these diverse subjects are constituents of one unified discipline. The second book is an anthology organized around various approaches to the study of well-being. These approaches focus on different aspects of well-being, such as emotion, cognition, the self, interpersonal factors, biological factors, coping mechanisms and personal strengths (Snyder and Lopez 2005). Once again, these all seem like intuitively promising ways to study well-being. But it is not clear why they form one coherent field of study.

The hypothesis that Positive Psychology is the study of PCNs explains the unity underlying the apparent disorder. Individual PCNs are complex, typically made up of many different sorts of states. And PCNs can be multiply realized: The states that comprise two people's PCNs might be quite different. The states that make up the well-being of the 25-year-old athlete will be different from those that make up the well-being of the spritely octogenarian. Psychologists tend to focus on PCNs at the cause-and-effect level, where feelings, emotions, attitudes, traits, and worldly interactions bump into each other. And this is all to the good. It is only by zeroing in on the details that we can come to understand the fine structure and dynamics of PCNs. If psychologists are studying PCNs, then of course they would study a wide array of states, such as pleasure, happiness, positive thinking, character strengths, values, interests, wellness, positive relationships, and so forth. These are typical components of PCNs. And of course they would study enabling institutions—institutions that tend to foster or inhibit such networks. And of course they would adopt a wide variety of approaches—studying people from the perspective of biological factors or their strengths, emotions, cognitions, self-conceptions, interpersonal relationships, or coping strategies—all of which are reasonable ways to investigate PCNs and PCN fragments.

There is an old yarn about six people groping in the dark to plumb the nature of an elephant: The tusk was thought a spear, the side a wall, the trunk a snake, the leg a tree, the ear a fan, and the tail a rope. This analogy is not apt for the psychology of well-being because psychologists are not groping in the dark to describe PCNs. A better analogy would have the six people studying the elephant in the dark with powerful but tightly focused flashlights. It is only when we step back and turn on the overhead lights that the higher-level pattern emerges.

2. The Structure of Positive Causal Networks

For the rest of this chapter, my goal is to demonstrate how PCNs organize and make sense of Positive Psychology. My contention is that the network theory is a framework that is already implicit in the science of well-being. It is not an alien system I am imposing from some abstract philosophical realm. So describing Positive Psychology from the perspective of the network theory should look a lot like simply describing Positive Psychology.

Some people feel and think and behave in ways that lead them to have a certain kind of success (for example, with friends, with a partner, with work), and this success leads them to feel, think, and behave in certain ways, which in turn fosters further success, and so on. These people are in a positive groove or cycle. They instantiate a positive causal network. The lion's share of Positive Psychology today involves the study of the *structure* of PCNs. These studies measure, identify, or manipulate one potential component of PCNs in order to discover its correlates, its causes, and its effects. My goal is to sketch some of what psychologists have discovered about the structure of PCNs in three different domains of life: friendship, intimate relationships, and work. This way of organizing the literature is artificial because these life domains do not come with their own independent PCNs. The networks inevitably overlap. The repetition of certain themes will reflect this overlap.

2.1. Friends

It is best to represent positive causal networks visually rather than with the written word. Most of the items that appear in Figure 4.1 are familiar to common sense, except perhaps for Positive Affect. (I take the "Positive Affect" link to represent

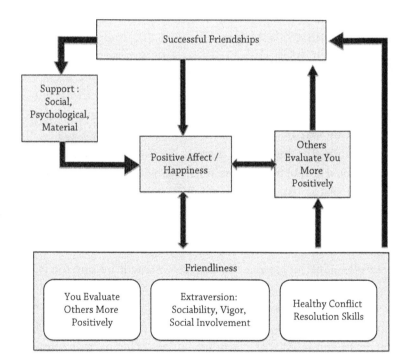

FIGURE 4.1

The Friendship Network

both a relatively stable disposition to have positive experiences as well as the occurrence of transient positive experiences. While this amalgam is conceptually unlovely, it helps keep things simple.)

It is best to understand the chart in Figure 4.1 as an idealization rather than as a representation of a real PCN. Real PCNs are messy and complicated. The arrows represent causal connections, often indirect ones that can be mediated in different ways. Despite the chart's imperfections, my contention is that there is enough evidence to suppose that something like this causal network exists even if some of its pieces should not survive further investigation.

The visual representation of this positive causal network makes clear that it is, in fact, a *network*, involving links bound together with many causal connections. The network consists of many positive cycles—connections that loop back onto the same types of states. Begin at any node and a sequence of causal connections will take you to any other node. As a result, and this can be lost in any linear written description, there is no compulsory starting point. There is no state we *must* privilege as the most important in the network. Mind you, there might *be* some states that are of particular importance to this network. But these questions go to the heart of the *dynamics* of PCNs rather than their *structure*. Dynamical questions concern what factors scuttle, inhibit, maintain, strengthen, or establish positive causal networks. Such questions will be our focus in section 3.

A good way to introduce the friendship network is by focusing on one of its core cycles. When positive affect is induced in the laboratory, studies suggest that it will tend to make you more sociable and friendly (Positive Affect → Friendliness) (Figure 4.2). For example, you are more likely to initiate a conversation with a stranger (Isen 1970) and offer

FIGURE 4.2

The Positive Affect–
Friendliness Cycle

intimate self-disclosures (Cunningham 1988). Induced positive affect makes you more generous in your judgments and interpretations of other people (Baron 1987). But this is in the lab. What about people who are naturally happy and not merely happy as a result of laboratory manipulations? They tend to judge their interactions with others to be more pleasant and enjoyable. For example, happier people are more likely to express a desire to be friends with or work on a project with a new acquaintance, and they are more likely to judge the person to be "kind, self-assured, open, tolerant, warm" (Lyubomirsky and Tucker 1998, 179). Might this be because happier people are less discriminating in their judgments of others? Apparently not. Happy and unhappy people give the same likability ratings to their new acquaintances (Lyubomirsky and Tucker 1998, 177). The generosity of happy people has practical implications. Students might be interested to know that happy faculty tend to write more positive letters of recommendation than unhappy faculty (Judge and Higgins 1998, 217).

Positive affect can also improve people's ability to cooperatively negotiate disagreements, an important skill for maintaining healthy relationships (Positive Affect → Friendliness). After a provocation, inducing positive affect lowers anger and hostility (Baron 1977, 1984). It predisposes people to healthier, more constructive conflict resolution strategies (Baron et al. 1990, 141). But the mechanics of conflict resolution are complex. Positive affect does not always promote cooperation. Baron et al. (1990) paired participants with partners with whom they would negotiate. The partners, who were part of the study, engaged in behaviors known to boost positive affect (a small gift, flattery, self-deprecating comments). The behaviors did not significantly change women's conflict resolution preferences, but they did raise men's preference for collaboration to that of women! One take-home message of this study is that affect-boosting behaviors that usually make people more cooperative tend to backfire right before tough negotiations, perhaps because they are readily interpreted as being manipulative.

Figure 4.3 represents another cycle that is important to the friendship network. The good vibes happy people send out to others are reciprocated in spades (Positive Affect → Others Judge One More Positively). People high in self-reported positive affect are more favorably judged by the people they interact with as well as by third parties (Berry and Hansen 1996, 800). A review

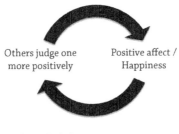

FIGURE 4.3

The Positive Affect–Others Judge
One More Positively Cycle

of the literature reports that happy people are judged to be better looking, more competent and intelligent, friendlier and more assertive, more moral "and even more likely to go to heaven." The friends and family of happier people judge them to be more "socially skilled (e.g., more articulate and well mannered), better public speakers, self-confident, and assertive, and as having more close friends, a strong romantic relationship, and more family support" (Lyubomirsky, King, and Diener 2005, 827, see text for citations).

Our discussion of friendship has focused on positive affect, but keep in mind that PCNs have no compulsory starting points. We could have started our discussion with the personality trait *extraversion*. In a longitudinal study, Costa and McCrae found that extraversion (e.g., sociability, vigor, social involvement) predicts positive affect and life satisfaction 10 years later (1980, 675) (Extraversion [Friendliness] → Positive Affect). In a meta-analysis (a statistical analysis of a large number of independent studies), DeNeve and Cooper (1998) argue that the extraversion–happiness correlation is quite strong; in fact, they argue for the existence of a PCN involving positive affect, friendly personality traits, and successful relationships.

> Positive affect is not tied solely to Extraversion. Rather, positive affect stems primarily from our connections with others, both in terms of the quantity of relationships (Extraversion) as well as the quality of relationships (Agreeableness) . . . [R]elationship type personality traits foster better relationships. However, they appear to provide another bonus to the holder; they also facilitate the experience of positive affect (220–221).

At the risk of beating a long dead horse, I am not imposing PCNs on psychology from the armchair. It's right there. DeNeve and

Cooper argue that positive affect brings about extraversion, which brings about more and stronger relationships, which brings about positive affect . . . and so on.

In a fascinating longitudinal study, Headey and Wearing (1989) interviewed hundreds of participants four times over six years (in 1981, 1983, 1985, 1987). They found that extraversion predicts life satisfaction and positive affect years later (736). This is precisely what we should expect given the existence of a PCN involving friendship. People who are better at making friends today are likely to be happier and more satisfied with their lives tomorrow. Headey and Wearing also took life event surveys. They asked participants to examine a list of favorable and adverse life events and check off how many they had experienced in some recent stretch of time. Here is what they found:

1. Elevated favorable events at time 1 predict elevated favorable events at time 2.
2. Elevated adverse events at time 1 predict elevated adverse events at time 2.
3. Elevated favorable events at time 1 predict somewhat elevated adverse events at time 2.

We should expect (1) if self-maintaining PCNs exist. And (2) suggests the existence of negative or vicious causal networks. But (3) is puzzling. If PCNs exist, then why do people with more than their fair share of favorable events today tend to have more than their fair share of adverse events in the future? This puzzle disappears upon closer inspection. Headey and Wearing explained this pattern of evidence in terms of people's age, openness to experience, extraversion and neuroticism (735).

A. More favorable and more adverse events are negatively correlated with age: So younger people tend to report more than their fair share of both favorable and adverse events.

B. More favorable and more adverse events are positively correlated with openness to experience: So people who are more open to experience tend to report more than their fair share of both favorable and adverse events.

C. Extraversion is positively correlated with favorable events but is not correlated with adverse events: So extraverts tend to have more than their fair share of favorable events but no more or less than their fair share of adverse events.

D. Neuroticism is positively correlated with adverse events but is not correlated with favorable events: So neurotics tend to have more than their fair share of adverse events but no more or less than their fair share of favorable events.

The puzzle, it seems, can be explained by (A) and (B): More favorable events at time 1 are correlated with youth and openness to experience, which are also correlated with more adverse events at time 2. (C) supports the idea there are positive causal networks involving extraversion and favorable events. Further support for believing positive friendship networks exist comes from a closer analysis of the *kinds* of positive and negative events that tend to be correlated over time. Events related to health tend to have rather low over-time correlations. So having more than one's fair share of positive health events at time 1 is not a strong predictor of positive health events at time 2. But people with more than their fair share of favorable friendship events at time 1 tend to be more extraverted and tend to have more than their fair share of favorable friendship events at time 2. This is exactly what we would predict if positive friendship networks exist. There is also evidence here for a positive professional success network (see section 2.3): positive job-related events are correlated with extraversion and with future positive job related events (735).[1]

2.2. Intimate Relationships

Psychology and common sense tell us that "happiness is consistently related to successful involvement with people" (Wilson 1967, 304). We have looked at friendship, so let's turn to love. Figure 4.4 is a visual representation of the positive relationship network with all the previous disclaimers still in effect (i.e., the chart is an idealized, incomplete empirical hypothesis).

Without any recourse to science, most of this chart appeals to common sense. Some people have healthy relationship skills and habits—they are effective at establishing emotional intimacy and enjoy that intimacy; they trust their partners and are generous toward them; and they are able to give and receive support and comfort in their relationships. Such people are more likely to enjoy healthy, fulfilling relationships. And a fulfilling relationship brings in its wake a whole host of benefits, which can make one generally happier and better adjusted. Being happier and more adjusted can play a role in other positive networks not included here, but these states can also foster better relationship skills and habits. The basic building blocks of the causal story are clear, and the causal story makes sense no matter where you begin. What we have here is the outline of a complex

1. A brief aside on the life event portion of this study. One might object that people's reports of positive and adverse events might have been tainted. Perhaps being happier makes one more inclined to remember or report on favorable events. To handle this objection, Headey and Wearing distinguished between life events "that it is difficult to believe anyone could forget or misperceive" (e.g., marriage, divorce, death of a loved one) and life events that are more likely to be subject to reporting errors (e.g., made lots of new friends) (734). The longitudinal correlations reported above held for both kinds of life events. So it is unlikely that these correlations are entirely the result of memory or reporting effects.

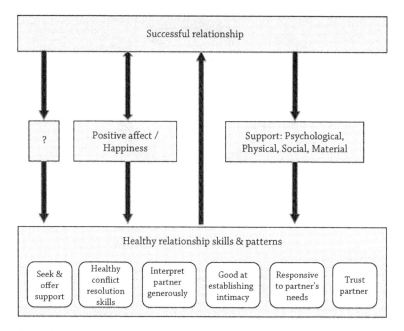

FIGURE 4.4

The Relationship Network

PCN—a cascading set of processes that ultimately loop back on the same sorts of states and so tend to be self-maintaining and mutually reinforcing.

The core of the relationship network (Figure 4.5) is an instance of Fredrickson's Broaden and Build Hypothesis (2001). Positive emotions give rise to "broadened" thought-action repertoires. In this case, it prompts one to be a better partner—more open, generous, responsive, and trusting. And being a better partner tends to lead to better relationships, which in turn leads to more positive emotions. There are three possible pairings of these three nodes, and for each pairing, there is strong evidence of mutual causal dependence. A discussion of the causal cycle involving positive affect and healthy relationship skills would

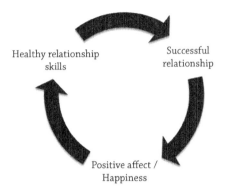

FIGURE 4.5

The Core of the Relationship Network

largely repeat much of our discussion of the friendship network. This is a reminder that the networks involving intimate relationships and friendship are bound to overlap. Let's turn to the cycle involving happiness and successful relationships (Figure 4.6).

It will surprise no one that one of the most robust findings in Positive Psychology is that people in satisfying relationships

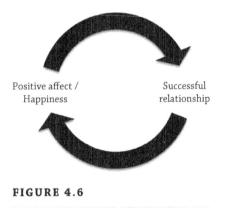

FIGURE 4.6

The PA–Relationship Cycle

tend to be happy (e.g., Diener and Seligman 2002). But the opposite is also true. People who are happier at one time will have happier marriages at a later time (e.g., Headey, Veenhoven, and Wearing 1991). In a striking study, Harker and Keltner (2001) examined the yearbook pictures of "a representative two thirds of" the senior classes of 1958 and 1960 at Mills College, a private women's college. They were looking for genuine Duchenne smiles, which involve the hard-to-fake "contraction of the orbicularis oculi muscle (i.e., the muscle surrounding the eyes) and results in raised cheeks, crow's-feet, and bagging under the eyes" (115). Thirty years later, Duchenne smilers were more likely to be married and more likely to be happily married (119). Needless to say, the connection between happiness at one time, or merely smiling genuinely for a yearbook picture, and marital happiness decades later is highly mediated. But this is precisely my point. The longitudinal evidence strongly suggests the existence of PCNs, of long-lasting causal networks that include both positive affect, and so a tendency toward Duchenne smiles when having ones picture snapped, and successful relationships.

There is strong evidence for a causal cycle involving successful relationships and healthy relationship skills (Figure 4.7). No one needs to be convinced that people with healthy relationship skills tend to have more successful relationships; and the opposite causal arrow might seem plausible as well. But the full breadth and power of these connections may not be obvious. The psychological literature bristles with different ways to assess relationship styles, skills, and habits. For example, Hazan and Shaver (1987) describe relationship styles that fit folk wisdom: Some people are too clingy (and worry too much about being abandoned), some are too stand-offish (uncomfortable with closeness, unsupportive, unwilling to trust their partners) and others are good at establishing closeness, enjoy it, expect partners to be trustworthy, turn to partners for comfort, and give

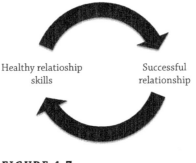

FIGURE 4.7

The Relationship–Relationship
Skills Cycle

comfort in return. Bartholomew and Horowitz (1991) have proposed an approach to understanding adult attachment styles in
terms of the person's views about themselves (positive or negative) and views about others (positive or negative). This suggests
four different attachment styles: secure (positive, positive), pre-
occupied (negative self, positive other), fearful or avoidant (negative self, negative other), and dismissing (positive self, negative
other). For any plausible way of assessing and measuring adult
relationship patterns, people with healthier relationship habits
tend to have more successful relationships. Peterson and Seligman (2004, 315) list some of the correlates of healthy attachment styles:

- more supportiveness and less rejection toward partners in
  joint problem-solving tasks (Kobak and Hazan 1991)
- safer sex practices (Brennan and Shaver 1995)
- fewer psychosomatic symptoms in response to stress (Mikulincer, Florian, and Weller 1993)
- greater likelihood of seeking support when distressed
  (Simpson, Rholes, and Nelligan 1992)

- using compromise (Pistole 1989) rather than destructive strategies (Gaines et al. 1997) of conflict resolution
- less deterioration of trust in the initial phases of relationship development (Keelan, Dion, and Dion 1994)
- higher self-esteem (Brennan and Bosson 1998)
- less depression (Carnelley, Pietromonaco, and Jaffe 1994)
- less partner abuse (Dutton, Saunders, Starzomski, and Bartholomew 1994)
- and a lower divorce rate (Hazan and Shaver 1987).

Less intuitive, but just as important, is evidence that the causal arrow goes in the opposite direction. For those of us who perhaps have not always had the best relationship skills, it is comforting to know that simply being in a healthy relationship fosters healthy relationship attitudes, traits, and habits—especially if one's partner has healthy relationship skills (Crowell, Fraley, and Shaver 1999). What mediates this connection? We don't know all the mediators, as represented by the "?" node in Figure 4.4. But positive affect is a plausible hypothesis. Learning via emulation or trial-and-error might sometimes play a mediating role as well. Another possibility inspired by Frederickson's Broaden and Build Hypothesis is that people in a successful relationship typically benefit from various kinds of support—physical, psychological, social, material—that promote a kind of security that makes them more likely to be open, trusting, and emotionally engaged.

2.3. Professional and Academic Success

Professional success (as measured by factors such as professional attainment, income, autonomy, and satisfaction) has a host of fellow travelers: positive feelings (positive affect, flow), positive attitudes (cheerfulness), and character traits (extraversion and optimism). Supervisor evaluations are better predicted by a person's self-reported well-being than her self-reported job satisfaction (Wright and Cropanzano 2000, 91, see also Wright, Bonett, and Sweeney 1993, Wright and Bonett 1997). Good supervisor ratings are nice, but what is the cash value of happiness? In a meta-analysis of 286 empirical investigations involving older adults, Pinquart and Sörensen found that income is better predicted by a person's self-reported well-being than her level of education (2000, 192, 194). The hypothesis on offer is that these kinds of correlations are underwritten by PCNs. With the standard disclaimers still in effect (i.e., the chart is an idealized, incomplete, and provisional empirical hypothesis), I suggest that a professional success network might look something like Figure 4.8.

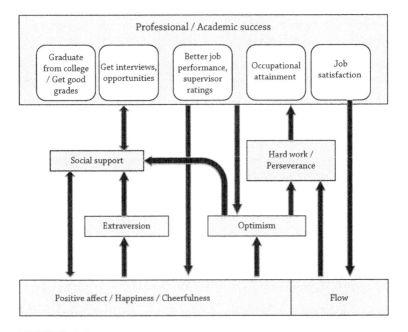

FIGURE 4.8

The Professional Success Network

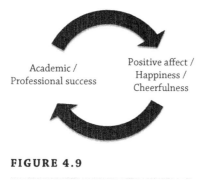

FIGURE 4.9

The Happiness–Success Cycle

At the heart of the professional success network is a happiness–success cycle (Figure 4.9). "The causal relationships suggest that happier individuals are more productive, and also that more productive individuals are happier. In short, affect and performance might be mutually reinforcing" (Côté 1999, 67).

In support of the bottom arrow, quality of life self-reports "predict academic retention both by itself and in conjunction with cumulative GPA 1 to 3 years in advance" (Frisch et al. 2005, 74). Happier people are more likely to get job interviews three months later (Burger and Caldwell 2000, 58). And in a fascinating longitudinal study involving over 13,000 participants, cheerfulness in the first year of college predicted job outcomes almost 20 years later.

> [I]ndividuals with a higher cheerfulness rating at college entry have a higher current income and a higher job satisfaction rating [20 years later] and are less likely ever to have been unemployed than individuals with a lower cheerfulness rating. Although cheerfulness generally has a positive effect on current income, this effect is curvilinear, with current income increasing more rapidly at lower than at higher cheerfulness

ratings; the effect is also moderated by parental income, with the increase in current income between any two cheerfulness ratings becoming greater as the level of parental income increases (Diener, Nickerson, Lucas, and Sandvik 2002, 248).

The income differences are dramatic. "[F]or individuals with average parental incomes . . . the difference in current income between those with the highest rating of cheerfulness and those with the lowest is more than $15,000 a year" (252). For individuals whose parents had high incomes (over $50,000 in 1975), the average difference is $25,000 a year (243). The claim is not that if you (somehow) dramatically boost your cheerfulness this will boost your earnings by hundreds of thousands of dollars over the course of your life. The right conclusion to draw is that there is some sort of stable underlying pattern that explains why the most cheerful college students tend to go on to make more money. Perhaps it's as simple as majors with less earning power tend to attract gloomier students, in which case, boosting your cheerfulness in college will not expand your earning potential. But the hypothesis on offer is that part of the reason for this long-term correlation is that positive causal networks have inertia. College students who have robust PCNs tend to become working adults who have robust PCNs.

In another longitudinal study, Roberts, Caspi, and Moffitt also found a happiness–professional success cycle (2003). They collected personality measures of 921 New Zealanders at ages 18 and 26, as well as a host of work outcomes at age 26 (e.g., prestige, educational level, earnings, power, work satisfaction, financial security). Happiness at 18 predicted professional success at 26. Those who scored high on positive emotionality at 18 had, compared to their cohort, "achieved work success, experienced fewer financial problems, and were happier in their jobs. They also acquired more stimulating work by age 26" (590). In addition, those who had achieved greater professional success had become "more socially dominant, hard working, and happier in the transition from adolescence to young adulthood" (588). Professional success is not a panacea. While work autonomy was associated with increases in happiness and well-being, it was also associated with increases in alienation (589).

What mediates the causal loop involving professional success and positive emotion? Staw, Sutton, and Pelled articulate some of the processes that underwrite the "positive emotion → professional success" connection.

> The model suggests that positive emotion brings about favorable outcomes on the job through three sets of intervening processes. First, positive emotion has desirable effects independent of a person's relationship with others, including greater task activity, persistence, and enhanced cognitive functioning. Second, people with positive rather than negative emotion benefit from more favorable responses by others. People with positive emotion are more successful at influencing others. They are also more likable, and a halo effect may occur when warm or satisfied employees are rated favorably on other desirable attributes. Third, people with positive feelings react more favorably to others, which is reflected in greater altruism and cooperation with others. We hypothesize that the combination of these intervening processes leads to favorable outcomes in the workplace, including achievement . . . job enrichment . . . and a more supportive social context. (1994, 52).

And then for good measure, they set these processes out in a chart (Figure 4.10). Add one more arrow, "Favorable Employee Outcomes at Work → Positive Emotion at Work," and what they have identified is a PCN.

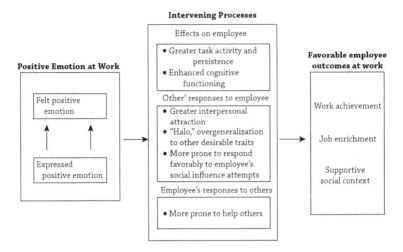

FIGURE 4.10

Professional Success and Positive Emotion

Reprinted by permission, Barry M. Staw, Robert I. Sutton, Lisa H. Pelled, "Employee Positive Emotion and Favorable Outcomes at the Workplace," *Organization Science* 5(1): 51–71. 1994, the Institute for Operations Research and the Management Sciences (INFORMS), Catonsville, MD.

Common sense tells us that strong social skills are an advantage in the workplace. The professional success network overlaps with the friendship and relationship networks. We've already seen studies in which extraversion predicts favorable "job-related events" years later; and having more than one's fair share of favorable job-related events at one time predicts more than one's fair share of favorable job-related events at later times (Headey and Wearing 1989, 735). And we've already looked at studies in which people high in positive affect tend to be better liked and treated more generously by others. This is true in the workplace as well. In an 18-month longitudinal study, Staw, Sutton, and Pelled found that happier people, as measured by self-report and an observer's record of "how often the employee smiled, laughed or said something funny," received more "emotional and tangible assistance" from their supervisors and their coworkers (1994, 60). Recall from our discussion of the relationship network, people with high positive affect tend to be more cooperative and less likely to engage in unhealthy conflict resolution. This is true in the workplace as well. A survey of CEOs and top managers of 62 U.S. companies found that management teams with high positive affect had "relatively higher levels of cooperativeness and lower levels of task and emotional conflict" (Barsade et al. 2000, 825). We might wonder whether the managers' happiness helps foster their organizational success or whether their organizational success helps foster their happiness. I would expect the causal arrow to run in both directions.

2.4. PCN Fragments

Most Positive Psychology research articles identify PCN fragments rather than full PCNs. I want to focus on a few particularly interesting fragments.

2.4.1. Creativity and Positive Affect

In a series of studies, Alice Isen and her colleagues have shown that inducing positive affect makes people more creative problem solvers. In one study, participants were given 10 minutes to solve Duncker's Candle Task: "the subject is presented with a box of tacks, a candle, and a book of matches and is asked to attach the candle to the wall (a corkboard) in such a way that it will burn without dripping wax on the table or floor" (Isen, Daubman, and Nowicki 1987, 1123). The trick is to make use of the box containing the tacks: Tack the box into the corkboard and place the candle in the box, which captures the dripping wax. In this study, 75% of subjects who had seen a funny film (9/12) gave the correct solution, compared to only 20% of the control subjects (3/15). In another study, positive affect subjects gave the correct solution 58% of the time (11/19), whereas participants in other conditions (some watched an upsetting film, others a neutral film, and yet others did two minutes of exercise) gave the correct solution no more than 30% of the time (1987, 1125).

Why does positive affect seem to make people more creative? We don't know, but Isen and her colleagues speculate:

> [G]ood feelings increase the tendency to combine material in new ways and to see relatedness between divergent stimuli. We hypothesize that this occurs because the large amount of cognitive material cued by the positive affective state results in defocused attention, and the more complex cognitive context thus experienced by persons who are feeling happy allows them a greater number and range of interpretations. This increased range of interpretations results in awareness of more aspects of stimuli and more possible ways of relating and combining them (1987, 1130).

Whatever the mechanism that explains the positive affect–creativity causal link, it would not be surprising for it to play a role in many PCNs.

2.4.2. Optimism and Success

Martin Seligman gives an account of optimism in terms of a person's explanatory style (1990). Pessimists tend to explain bad events in terms of factors that are permanent, pervasive, and personal, whereas optimists tend to explain bad events in terms of factors that are temporary, specific to this occasion, and not their fault but rather the result of luck or circumstance. When it comes to good events, the situation is reversed (1990, 44–49). Studies show correlations between optimism and professional success (Seligman and Schulman 1986), academic success in college (Peterson and Barrett 1987), and athletic performance (Seligman et al. 1990).

> Literally hundreds of studies show that pessimists give up more easily and get depressed more often. These experiments also show that optimists do much better in school and college, at work and on the playing field. They regularly exceed the predictions of aptitude tests. When optimists run for office, they are more apt to be elected than pessimists are. Their health is unusually good. They age well, much freer than most of us from the usual physical ills of middle age. Evidence suggests they may even live longer (1990, 4–5).

Seligman proposes a framework for understanding these results that appeals to a feedback loop that is probably part of many PCNs.

> Common sense tells us that success makes people optimistic. But . . . we have seen repeatedly that the arrow goes in the opposite direction as well. Optimistic people become successes. In school, on the playing field, and at work, the optimistic individual makes the most of his talent (Seligman 1990, 255).

What we have here are persistent but not inevitable cycles of optimism and accomplishment that people generally value and enjoy despite the inevitable setbacks and frustrations. What we have, in other words, are fragments of positive causal networks.

2.4.3. Healthy Coping and Positive Affect

Coping styles are the characteristic ways that people deal with stressful or difficult situations (Moos 1988, Carver et al. 1989). Fredrickson and Joiner asked people to fill out self-report instruments that measure affect and coping on two different occasions, five weeks apart (2002, 173). Higher levels of positive affect predicted a healthier coping style five weeks later. This result fits with the findings that positive affect promotes more positive, creative, and expansive thinking. They also identified the second side of the positive cycle: A healthier coping style predicted improvement in positive affect five weeks later. Interestingly, they did not find a relationship between low negative affect and healthier coping style. Low negative affect did not improve future healthier coping styles. And healthier coping styles did not reduce negative affect. What is crucial to the "upward spiral" is feeling good, not simply not feeling bad (173). "Individuals who experienced more positive emotions than others became more resilient to adversity over time, as indexed by increases in broad-minded coping. In turn, these enhanced coping skills predicted increased positive emotions over time" (Fredrickson 2001, 223–224). This spiral of positive affect and improved ability to cope with tough situations is likely to play a role in many different PCNs.

2.4.4. Engagement and Positive Affect

Happier people tend to be more engaged with the world (Costa and McCrae 1980, Kozma and Stones 1983, Headey and Wearing 1989, Burger and Caldwell 2000), and people who are more engaged with the world tend to be healthier and happier (Diener and Seligman 2002). Fredrickson and Branigan (2005) showed people film clips designed to induce various emotions. They were then "asked to step away from the specifics of the film" and were given the following instruction:

> . . . take a moment to imagine being in a situation yourself in which this particular emotion would arise. . . . Concentrate on all the emotion you would feel and live it as vividly and as deeply as possible. *Given this feeling*, please list all the things you would like to do *right now* (320).

Participants were given a page with 20 blank lines that began with the phrase "I would like to _____." After five minutes, positive affect subjects had listed significantly more actions than the control (neutral film) subjects and the negative affect subjects. Compared to the neutral subjects, the positive affect subjects more often expressed a desire to engage in active outdoor or sporting activities and less often expressed a desire to rest or sleep. On the other hand, compared to the neutral subjects, the negative affect subjects expressed fewer desires to eat, drink, reminisce, or work. Those who saw the anger-inducing film expressed more urges to be anti-social and fewer urges to read, whereas those who saw the anxiety-inducing film reported more urges "to affiliate with others" (325). This engagement cycle is likely to be part of many PCNs.

2.4.5. Altruism and Happiness

There is a relatively large literature showing a strong correlation between volunteering and various positive life outcomes, greater life satisfaction, less depression and anxiety, and superior physical health and longevity (e.g., Borgonovi 2008, Meier and Stutzer 2008, Post 2005). The hard-nosed skeptic might doubt whether altruism and happiness are mutually reinforcing. But we have already considered evidence that positive affect promotes friendliness, cooperation, more favorable attitudes toward others, and healthier coping styles. So it wouldn't be surprising if it also promoted altruistic behavior. Isen found that subjects who were told they were successful in a task, a standard method for inducing positive affect, were more likely to donate to a charity or help a stranger who had dropped a book (Isen 1970). In a classic study that has received quite a bit of philosophical attention (e.g., Doris 2002), when a person dropped a folder of papers in front of subjects, 87% of subjects (14/16) who had found a dime in a phone booth stopped to help, whereas only 4% of subjects (1/25) who had not found a dime stopped to help (Isen and Levin 1972). In the same study, subjects who were given cookies were more likely to volunteer their time. So there is strong evidence that folks who are happier tend to be more altruistic. What about the opposite? Does altruism tend to make folks feel better? There is some evidence that, yes, it does.

Thoits and Hewitt (2001) interviewed a large sample of people three years apart. They found the expected half of the causal loop: "people who were happier, more satisfied with their lives, higher in self-esteem, in good health, and low in depression at Time 1 worked significantly more volunteer hours at Time 2" (124). And they found the other half of the causal loop as well: "volunteer work hours in the last twelve months significantly enhance all six aspects of well-being at the Time 2 interview. . . . These effects of volunteerism hold even after individuals' participation in other voluntary groups and their prior levels of personal well-being have been controlled. In short, volunteer service is beneficial to personal well-being independent of other forms of religious and secular community participation" (126). Thoits and Hewitt explicitly make the case for this being a "positive cycle" (127). Happier people volunteer and volunteering makes people happier.

2.4.6. Positive Affect and the Own Race Bias

The Own Race Bias is people's tendency to recognize and distinguish people of their own race better than people of other races. Despite its shameful past, this "They all look the same to me" phenomenon is not the exclusive province of the ignorant or the racist. Measures of prejudice, both implicit and explicit prejudice, are not correlated with the Own Race Bias (Ferguson et al. 2001, 567). What's more, hours of intensive training only reduces the Own Race Bias for a short time. A week later, the training makes no difference (Lavrakas, Buri, and Mayzner 1976).

Johnson and Fredrickson (2005) explored how inducing various emotions affects the Own Race Bias. White participants were shown 28 faces in random order, and then they were shown in random order 56 faces (the same 28 faces and 28 new faces). The faces were evenly divided between race and gender. People who had seen a funny film clip recognized white and black faces at the same rate, whereas people who had seen film clips of a horror movie or of non-emotional material did not. Positive affect made the Own Race Bias disappear. Johnson and Fredrickson offer various potential explanations for this (875–879). One possible cause of the Own Race Bias is that while face recognition tends to be efficient because we recognize faces holistically—"as a collective whole instead of a collection of parts" (875)—cross-race faces may be perceived less holistically than own-race faces. Positive emotions are known to produce more holistic, "global" thinking, and so may promote more holistic perceptions of cross-race faces. They do not lead to superior perceptions of own-race faces because of a ceiling effect: Own-race faces are already recognized about as efficiently as they can be. Now, the Own Race Bias result is a very specific finding, and it would be a mistake to make too much of it. But in conjunction with the altruism cycle, it raises an optimistic possibility. Societies might be better off in unexpected ways if more people could be enmeshed in robust PCNs.

2.4.7. Curiosity and Knowledge

Despite its purported lethal effect on felines, curiosity is generally good for people. There is evidence for a self-maintaining curiosity-knowledge cycle: People who are more curious about a domain of knowledge learn more about it. This is obvious enough. A number of studies suggest that the opposite is also true. People who learn more about a domain of knowledge tend to become more curious about it. In one study, participants were asked to rate how curious they were about questions concerning invertebrate animals. People tended to be more curious about invertebrate animals they were more familiar with (Berlyne 1954). Another study found that while general knowledge did not correlate with curiosity, there was a correlation between knowledge about a particular issue and curiosity: "subjects were more curious toward items about which they already had some knowledge than toward those about which they had little or no knowledge" (Jones 1979, 640). In another study, participants were asked about the most northern, southern, and western state (but not the easternmost state) in the United States. There were four groups distinguished by (a) whether or not they had been asked to guess about the northern, southern, and western states, and (b) whether they had been given accurate feedback. So there were four groups:

1. Non-guessers with no feedback.
2. Non-guessers with feedback.

3. Guessers with no feedback.
4. Guessers with feedback.

Only the fourth group, the group that guessed and received feedback, were more curious than average to learn which state is easternmost in the United States (Loewenstein et al. 1992). The active acquisition of knowledge, even if it only involves guessing and feedback, boosts curiosity.

3. The Dynamics of Positive Causal Networks

Once we have a handle on the structure of PCNs, it is natural to ask which comes "first"—the thinking, the feeling, the accomplishment, or something else? What factors tend to establish, maintain, or strengthen these positive networks? What factors tend to destroy them? These are questions about the *dynamics* of PCNs and they represent Positive Psychology's normative aspiration. This aspiration is explicit in two definitions we considered earlier: "Positive Psychology aims to help people live and flourish rather than merely to exist" (Keyes and Haidt 2003, 3) and "The label of *Positive Psychology* represents those efforts of professionals to help people optimize human functioning" (Wright and Lopez 2005, 42). While psychologists have tentatively identified a number of interventions that promote or enhance well-being, we don't really know how or why they work. And of course these findings are hostage to future discoveries. But the network theory is not committed to the effectiveness of any particular interventions, including the ones described below. It is only committed to the thesis that Positive Psychology is, in part, the study of the dynamics of PCNs. It seeks to identify factors that scuttle, inhibit, maintain, strengthen, or establish PCNs.

3.1. Dynamical Distinctions

We can make some natural distinctions about the dynamics of PCNs.

1. *Prerequisites.* Prerequisites are necessary for any PCNs to exist at all or to exist with any moderate degree of strength. Their absence destroys or dramatically degrades every PCN. Prerequisites for well-being plausibly include minimal resources and some degree of security, physical health, and mental health. So, for example, without physical health, it is very difficult to be in a robust PCN relating to friendship or professional success. That's not to say that someone who is ill cannot have friends. Our friends can make our lives better when we're very sick, but a debilitating or painful illness can make it difficult or impossible to enter into a robust PCN. Physical health is a prerequisite for well-being. It does not bring about any particular PCNs. It just makes PCNs possible.

2. *Essentials.* An essential link is a state that is necessary for the operation of some range of positive causal networks. The absence of an essential link scuttles a PCN or a significant part of a PCN. But it is unlike a prerequisite because its absence does not undermine the possibility of having any PCNs at all.

The difference between essentials and prerequisites can be tricky. Whether something is a prerequisite for well-being is a *general* fact about the dynamics of human well-being. It is a general fact that having enough to eat and drink is a prerequisite for well-being (i.e., for having any PCNs whatsoever). Suppose Bill identifies with his work to such a degree that it is practically impossible for him to have a PCN in absence of professional success. Professional success is not a prerequisite for well-being, as people can have well-being without it. But it is essential to *Bill's* well-being, to his being able to have a PCN at all. Because professional success is a necessary link for only a proper subset of PCNs, it is not a prerequisite for well-being. And so it is not a prerequisite for Bill's well-being, even if Bill must have professional success in order to pull off any PCN at all. One way to think about the robustness of a PCN is in terms of its essentials. Bill's PCN is less robust because professional success is essential to it. To put it another way, if professional success were not essential to Bill's PCN, if it could survive in modified form without the professional success, his PCN would be more robust.

Now let's turn to the causal drivers of PCNs, the conditions that tend to bring about PCNs.

3. *Enhancers*. An enhancer is a state that tends to strengthen an existing PCN. For example, a raise might enhance Bill's well-being by strengthening (i.e., making more robust) his work-related PCN. But the raise might not be essential to maintaining the PCN.

4. *Promoters*. A promoter is a state that is typically or practically sufficient to establish a PCN. Insofar as we want to improve people's lives, identifying promoters is important. It is in principle possible to rate the effectiveness of a promoter along three dimensions.

   a. *Breadth*: The breadth of the promoter is the number of environments in which it tends to work, in which it tends to establish PCNs.

   b. *Efficiency*: The efficiency of the promoter is how likely it is to work in a particular kind of environment.

   c. *Power*: The power of the promoter is a function of the strength (robustness) of the networks it tends to produce when it produces them.

Obviously, it would be ideal to discover promoters that have great breadth, efficiency, and power: They produce highly robust networks for most people in most environments. But of course not every promoter will be ideally effective.

The distinction between promoters and enhancers is clearer in theory than in practice. Psychologists have discovered interventions that lead to long-term, stable improvements in various measures of well-being. Are these promoters or enhancers of well-being? Or perhaps both? It is typically hard to tell. I have found nothing in the literature resembling the distinction. Perhaps it is not useful in the field. Or perhaps we just don't understand the dynamics of PCNs well enough yet to draw such fine distinctions. So my plan is to be rather cavalier in discussing the causal drivers of PCNs, states that bring about well-being. It is enough for the network theory that Positive Psychology studies interventions that improve a person's well-being by either establishing new PCNs or strengthening existing PCNs.

3.2. The Dynamics of Ill-Being

Boosting our well-being is only half the story about how we can improve our lives. We can also make our lives better by getting out of the state of ill-being. I have resolutely avoided this point until now. One might try to defend a network theory of ill-being, explaining it in terms of negative causal networks and fragments of such networks. But properly defending a theory of ill-being would be a large undertaking, well beyond the scope of this work. Even so, to fully account for the ways we can improve our lives, we would need both a theory of well-being and a theory of ill-being. And as I have suggested, at least some instances of ill-being involve negative or vicious causal networks. Consider, for example, the cognitive model of panic attacks. As the name implies, a panic attack is an attack of severe panic that typically lasts for some minutes and often includes palpitations, accelerated heart rate, sweating, trembling, dizziness, chest pain, or shortness of breath. Severe attacks can involve a sense of impending insanity or death. The cognitive model takes panic attacks to involve a vicious cycle of misinterpretation (Clark 1986). A person experiences sensations of anxiety and misinterprets them as symptoms of a much more dangerous episode, such as an impending heart attack. The misinterpretation produces greater feelings of anxiety, fear, and panic. These sensations are again misinterpreted as evidence, indeed stronger evidence, that some terrible event is about to occur. And so the vicious anxiety-misinterpretation cycle builds on itself. Depression often seems to involve vicious cycles of negative feelings and worldly failings (Teasdale 1988).

These examples do not support a full-blown causal network view of ill-being. But they do suggest that some instances of ill-being can be profitably understood along these lines, as having essential links (states that are usually or typically necessary for the continuation of ill-being networks), enhancers (states that strengthen networks of ill-being), and promoters (states that establish networks of ill-being). There is evidence that rumination is a promoter of depression. Rumination involves repetitively reflecting on the symptoms and potential causes of distress in a way that does not lead to active problem solving. Non-depressed ruminators are at high risk of becoming depressed (Nolen-Hoeksema, Wisco, and Lyubomirsky 2008). A promoter of ill-being need not also be an essential link. For example, once rumination has done its dirty work, avoiding rumination might not do much, if anything, to defeat the already established depressive cycle. The potential mismatch between promoters and essential links is crucial for overcoming ill-being, particularly for promoters we cannot avoid. Suppose there is a genetic promoter of ill-being—in a wide range of environments it tends to bring about a depression (Caspi 2003). We cannot avoid our genetic heritage. But suppose that, as proponents of cognitive therapy argue, certain negative habits of thought are essential links in many depressive cycles (Burns 1980). The hopeful upshot is that we can render promoters of ill-being ineffective by removing an essential link. So regardless of what promoters of depression might exist, they can be stymied by eliminating the negative habits of thought that are essential to the vicious cycle.

3.3. Improving Our Lives: The Dynamics of Well-Being and Ill-Being

Suppose an intervention brings about a long-term improvement in your life. It might work by promoting well-being (establishing or strengthening a PCN), defeating ill-being (removing an essential link of a negative causal network), or both. The distinction between promoters of well-being and defeaters of ill-being is easy to overlook. Just because an intervention is capable of establishing a robust PCN doesn't necessarily mean it is also capable of putting an end to a malady, and vice versa. This distinction between alleviating psychic distress and promoting well-being is often cited as a fundamental motivation for Positive Psychology (e.g., Seligman and Csikszentmihalyi 2000, Gable and Haidt 2005). The separate dynamics of well-being and ill-being also provide an explanation for how a person might have a high or low degree of both simultaneously.

Now let's turn to some examples of interventions that improve a person's life. There is evidence that a regimen of moderate exercise both defeats ill-being and promotes well-being. Moderate exercise brings a host of health benefits, including a longer life and lower rates of heart disease, hypertension, diabetes, osteoporosis, and various forms of cancer (Penedo and Dahn

2005). These are pretty obvious well-being prerequisites. There is also evidence that exercise alleviates at least some forms of ill-being, such as depression and anxiety disorders (2000). But for non-clinical populations, it appears that moderate exercise also helps bring about long-term improvements in mood and life evaluations (Moses et al. 1989, Hassmen, Koivula, and Uutela 2000, De Moor et al. 2006). There is still much we have to learn about exercise and the good life—how much is effective, why it is effective, and the ways it might backfire (Scully et. al 1998). Even with these qualifications, however, the research seems to support the idea that moderate exercise is capable of defeating ill-being and promoting well-being.

Psychologists seek to discover effective promoters of well-being. For example, Seligman, Steen, Park, and Peterson (2005) conducted a study to explore whether certain activities, performed over a week-long period, could lead to an improvement in self-reported well-being six months later. Visitors to a website devoted to Seligman's book, *Authentic Happiness*, were recruited, so this was a self-selected population. Participants were randomly assigned to perform one of the following exercises over the course of one week:

1. Placebo: Participants wrote about their early memories every night.
2. Gratitude Visit: Participants wrote and delivered a thank-you letter to someone they hadn't properly thanked.
3. Three Good Things: Every day, participants wrote down three good things that happened and explained why they happened.
4. You at Your Best: Participants wrote about a time they were at their best and reflected on the personal strengths displayed in that episode, and then reviewed the story every day.

5. Use Strengths: Participants took a survey that identified their five "signature strengths" and used those strengths every day.

6. Novel Use of Strengths: Participants took a survey that identified their five "signature strengths" and used those strengths in new and different ways every day.

Prior to being assigned to an exercise, and then again one week, one month, three months, and six months later, participants were surveyed to assess their states of depression and happiness.

Now comes the moment for you to test your empirical judgment: Which, if any, of the five happiness exercises had significantly better results than the placebo in increasing long-term happiness scores and reducing long-term depression scores? If you need a hint, it might be helpful to know that when the authors conducted a follow up, they discovered an interesting correlation: "We found that the participants who continued to benefit from the exercises were those people who spontaneously did them beyond the required one-week period, without our instruction to do so" (420). So which exercises do you think people would have been more likely to continue on their own? For one final hint, two of the exercises were not effective. One was effective immediately but its effectiveness wore off after one month. And two exercises were effective at improving happiness and depression scores for the entire six months.

The interventions that were not effective were You at Your Best and Use Strengths. The intervention that was effective for just one month was Gratitude Visit. And the interventions that had positive long-term effects on both depression and happiness scores were Three Good Things and Novel Use of Strengths. These are the two exercises that tended to stick—people continued to do them after the experimental intervention was over.

Why did people continue to do them? The authors speculate: "We believe that these two interventions involve skills that improve with practice, that are fun, and that thus are self-maintaining. Unlike many therapeutic outcomes, such as weight loss from dieting, these exercises are self-reinforcing" (420). (At this point, I wonder if it would test your patience to mention yet again that Positive Psychology is littered with evidence and speculations about PCNs. Perhaps I'll just mention it in a parenthetical comment.)

Psychologists have identified numerous interventions that improve people's lives. It is at least sometimes difficult to tease out whether these interventions defeat ill-being, promote well-being, or do both. I should mention one important class of studies. There is strong evidence that therapy alleviates certain forms of psychological distress (Smith and Glass 1977, Landman and Dawes 1982). For example, there is ample evidence that cognitive therapy can help some people overcome depression or anxiety disorders (for an opinionated review, see Bishop and Trout 2013). But once therapy has eliminated these maladies, can it then establish positive causal networks, that is, promote well-being? Given my reading of the evidence, the jury on this question is out.

4. The Well-Being of Groups

The network theory provides a natural way to think about the well-being of groups (e.g., families, organizations, businesses, nations). The study of group well-being is the study of the structure and dynamics of interpersonal PCNs. PCNs can range over more than a single person. The existence of interpersonal PCNs is implicit in the discussions of intrapersonal PCNs. In a healthy, active friendship, two people's feelings, emotions, attitudes, behaviors, and traits are bound up in a causal network. Anne is a rich source of emotional support for Samantha—evaluating her positively, doing small favors, making sure she's okay when she's sick or down, and giving support during the occasional crisis. Anne's actions, and even Samantha's knowledge that Anne is "there for her" (disposed to help even if Samantha doesn't need it), promote in Samantha a host of positive emotions, attitudes (e.g., friendliness), and abilities (e.g., better conflict resolution skills). These positive states in turn prompt Samantha to behave in ways that are supportive of Anne. And so Samantha and Anne are connected by a rich causal web, an interpersonal PCN, that should by now be familiar. For the network theory, the group consisting of Anne and Samantha has a high degree of well-being even if neither individual has a particularly high degree of well-being. I'm sure I'm not alone in having had the benefit of good friends through otherwise miserable times.

For the network theory, the well-being of a group is not simply an additive function of the well-being of its members. A family might be dysfunctional even if each member of the family is high in well-being. In that case, the intrapersonal PCNs of each member of the family would be very strong while the family's interpersonal PCN would be very weak or non-existent. Alternatively, a group might have a high degree of well-being even if the individuals who make up the group have only moderate degrees of well-being. Each group member would possess only PCN fragments, but those fragments would form a very strong interpersonal PCN. It's not possible for a group to have well-being when its members are entirely bereft of well-being. There can be no group well-being without the raw material to make up an interpersonal PCN. So there is bound to be a correlation between the well-being of groups and the well-being of their members. Not just because group well-being is composed of states that make up the PCNs (or PCN fragments) of individuals, but also because positive emotions, attitudes, and dispositions are contagious. People higher in well-being will tend to form healthier, more successful groups.

Attempts to characterize the study of group well-being tend to suffer from the same problems as attempts to characterize positive psychology.

> [Positive Organization Scholarship] focuses on the generative (that is, life-building, capability-enhancing, capacity-creating) dynamics in organizations that contribute to human strengths and virtues, resilience and healing, vitality and thriving, and the cultivation of extraordinary states in individuals, groups and organizations. [Positive Organization Scholarship] is premised on the belief that enabling human excellence in organizations unlocks latent potential and reveals hidden possibilities in people and systems that can benefit both human and organizational welfare (Dutton, Glynn, and Spreitzer 2006, 641).

This is a list of "for examples" liberally peppered with ill-defined but intuitively compelling terms. The problem with the description is not that it is inaccurate. The problem is that it fails to identify the scientific category studied by this discipline. My proposal is that the study of group well-being is the study of interpersonal PCNs.

The network theory provides a clear, non-distorting framework for understanding empirical research on group well-being. Consider an example. Spreitzer et al. (2005) identify three work-related contexts that tend to foster individual thriving among employees—decision-making discretion, information sharing, and a climate of trust and respect (Figure 4.11). Once the organization promotes individual thriving, this leads to

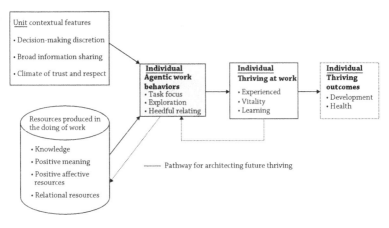

FIGURE 4.11

Group Well-Being and Positive Causal Networks

Reprinted by permission. Gretchen Spreitzer, Kathleen Sutcliffe, Jane Dutton, Scott Sonenshein, Adam M. Grant, "A Socially Embedded Model of Thriving at Work," *Organization* Science 16(5): 537–549. 2005, the Institute for Operations Research and the Management Sciences (INFORMS), Catonsville, MD.

positive "agentic" work behaviors, at least some of which involve positive relationships with other members of the organization. These positive behaviors, in turn, promote individual thriving, which in turn promotes positive behaviors. These positive behaviors also tend to produce resources—knowledge, positive meaning, positive affective resources, and positive relationships—which in turn promote those same kinds of positive behavior. This study identifies a set of tight-knit interpersonal PCNs that ground the operation of a thriving organization. Interpersonal PCNs are common denizens of the empirical literature on group well-being (e.g., Liang, Moreland, and Argote 1995, Cameron 2003, Cameron, Bright, and Caza 2004, Lewis, Lange, and Gillis 2005).

5. Conclusion

The network theory takes Positive Psychology to be the study of the structure and dynamics of positive causal networks (PCNs). My goal in this chapter has been to present six pieces of evidence for thinking that the network theory successfully organizes and makes sense of Positive Psychology.

1. Many psychologists have identified PCNs (though not under that description). Some have proposed interesting and important hypotheses concerning PCNs (though, again, not under that description).
2. The network theory provides a clear, concise, and accurate characterization of Positive Psychology: It is the study of the structure and dynamics of PCNs. This definition makes true the various characterizations offered by practitioners—the ones that use ill-defined but intuitively powerful terms, the ones that give non-exhaustive lists of examples, and the ones that do both. Each of these characterizations can be plausibly interpreted as expressing the basic idea that Positive Psychology is the study of PCNs.
3. The network theory provides a natural way to understand group well-being as the study of interpersonal PCNs.
4. The network theory organizes the various methods and approaches different researchers take to doing Positive Psychology. PCNs are complex and multiply realizable states. It is reasonable to take different approaches to the study of PCNs (biological, interpersonal, emotional, cognitive, etc.) and to focus on the various states that frequently appear in PCNs (positive affect, optimism, curiosity, relationship skills, health, longevity, etc.).
5. The network theory accurately describes a large portion of research in Positive Psychology as the study of the

structure of PCNs. These studies identify and describe the correlations and causal connections between positive feelings, moods, emotions, attitudes, dispositions (or traits), and objective factors (e.g., income, longevity, health, academic performance).

6. The network theory accurately describes an important and growing portion of research in Positive Psychology as the study of the dynamics of PCNs. These studies seek to identify the sorts of states that establish positive causal networks (promoters), that strengthen such networks (enhancers), that are required for particular networks (essential links), and that are required for any networks whatsoever (prerequisites).

This is the heart of the case for the network theory of well-being—its ability to organize and make sense of this psychological literature, a literature that is (intuitively) the empirical study of well-being. Any time the network theory is under pressure, I will come back to this point. Let me foreshadow.

• Some readers will object that the account of PCNs at the core of the theory is weak or problematic. In response, I will probably grant the charge, remind you that such infelicities are common early in the life of a successful scientific concept, and then argue that the network theory, despite its flaws, explains the evidence far better than any alternative theory of well-being (see chapter 5).

• Some readers will object that the network theory has counterintuitive implications: it takes someone to have well-being when common sense says she doesn't or it takes someone not to have well-being when common sense says she does. In response, I will probably grant the charge, note that every consistent theory of well-being has implications that *some* people find counterintuitive, remind you that many successful scientific concepts have counterintuitive results, and then argue that the network theory, despite its flaws, explains the totality of the evidence far better than any alternative theory of well-being (see chapter 5).

The network theory explains the scientific evidence. Now it's time to consider how it handles the evidence of common sense and how it fares against the competition.

Chapter 5

The Case for the Network Theory:
An Inference to the Best Explanation

[handwritten margin notes: "Explanatory Reasoning", "Who what where why when How", "Aristotle"]

The case for the network theory is an inference to the best explanation. The network theory explains the evidence better than its competitors. The competitors I will consider are the informed desire theory, the authentic happiness theory, Aristotle's theory, and hedonism. My strategy will be simple: Battle to a draw on common sense and win on the science. The network theory explains our commonsense judgments well enough to not be disqualified and it is so superior to its competitors at explaining the scientific evidence that it carries the day.

To run this argument, we need to figure out whose judgments will comprise the commonsense evidence our theories are supposed to explain. One way to proceed would be to run surveys to find out what folks think about well-being. But there is a simpler way. The inclusive approach asks us to take our commonsense judgments with a grain of salt. Without evidence to the contrary, our default view should be that our pre-scientific opinions about well-being are at least roughly accurate, but they might be somewhat mistaken. This means that as long as there is reasonable overlap in our well-being judgments, it doesn't matter whose judgments we use as our commonsense evidence. Suppose we use my commonsense judgments as evidence, and hedonism explains those judgments perfectly, but the informed desire theory only explains them reasonably well. This can't confirm hedonism and disconfirm the informed desire theory because we simply can't be confident enough in the accuracy of my commonsense judgments. A theory of well-being is in jeopardy from the commonsense evidence only if it does serious violence to that evidence. To capture this idea, let's say that a theory of well-being is a *live option* if it explains reasonably well the commonsense judgments of people who have a good grasp of our shared concept of well-being. People like you, like your neighbor, or like philosophers.

As it happens, philosophers have made it easy to figure out what they think about well-being. They have written thousands of pages mulling over their commonsense judgments and building theories that answer to those judgments. I propose to use philosophers as our source of commonsense who evidence. Not because their judgments are necessarily better than anyone else's, but because they're good enough and they're readily available.

By taking philosophers' commonsense judgments as evidence, I have given the four established theories a big head start in their competition with the upstart network theory. Those theories have been carefully honed and developed to capture the well-being judgments of philosophers. Not surprisingly, they do a good job of it. And so they start off as live options. My plan is to leverage this fact to show that the upstart is also a live option: The fact that the network theory sanctions philosophers' commonsense judgments about what is right and wrong with each live competitor theory is evidence that the network theory is also a live option. Philosophers accustomed to the traditional approach might find my treatment of the philosophical literature strange. I will articulate simple "vanilla" descriptions of the competitor theories and of the standard objections leveled at those theories. And I will ignore the many sophisticated moves and countermoves philosophers make in the literature. That's because I am not trying to show that the standard objections against these theories are *true*—although ultimately I do think many of them are true. What I am trying to show is that the network theory is a live option because it implies that philosophers' commonsense judgments about the competitor theories are true or at least plausible. As far as the commonsense evidence is concerned, the network theory is in the same boat as its competitors. They are all live options. Whether (say) the hedonist has a clever way to develop or revise her theory so that it avoids a standard objection doesn't much matter because that objection, based as it is on the commonsense evidence, isn't going to sink hedonism anyway.

After battling its competitors to a draw on the commonsense evidence, the network theory will win on the scientific evidence. The scientific evidence our five theories must explain is in the library, mostly in well-respected peer-reviewed journals. A theory of well-being will face two challenges in trying to make sense of the science. First, a theory must appeal to some state or states that psychologists study. No matter how intuitively plausible the theory might be, it can't explain the science if it doesn't connect with the science. This is the *fitting problem*: the challenge of fitting the central construct of a theory—pleasure, authentic happiness, desire satisfaction, virtues, positive causal networks—to the empirical literature. But connecting with the science isn't enough. As we saw in chapter 3, Positive Psychology appears to be an unorganized hodgepodge of different research projects. It lacks a clear, generally agreed upon definition. And it studies an exceptionally wide array of states from a number of

Network Theory is in the same as other theories

Some would argue

different perspectives. The *privileging problem* is the challenge of explaining the order behind the apparent disorder: How does the theory organize the startling diversity of research that flies under the banner of Positive Psychology?

The network theory provides straightforward, natural solutions to both the fitting and the privileging problems. It handles the fitting problem by explicitly taking its central construct from the empirical literature. (That, at least, was the idea.) Psychologists have been studying and theorizing about positive causal networks for years. The network theory solves the privileging problem by taking Positive Psychology to be the study of positive causal networks. It provides a framework for understanding Positive Psychology that (a) makes sense of the various definitions experts have offered for Positive Psychology; (b) provides a unified treatment of individual and group well-being (intrapersonal and interpersonal PCNs and PCN fragments); (c) explains why Positive Psychology studies so many different states from so many different perspectives (because PCNs can be realized in many different ways); (e) explains why Positive Psychology identifies and describes correlations and causal connections among the basic elements of PCNs (it studies the structure of PCNs); and (f) makes sense of what psychologists are doing when they study interventions that promote or inhibit well-being (they're studying the dynamics of PCNs).

The problem with hedonism, Aristotelianism, the informed desire theory, and the authentic happiness view is not that they fail to explain our commonsense judgments. They explain those judgments just fine. The problem is that they do not provide a framework that is as good as the network theory at organizing and making sense of the scientific literature. And until they do, we should accept the network theory as the best explanation of the evidence.

1. Hedonism

Hedonism about well-being is the thesis that a person's well-being is a function of the balance of her positively valenced experience (e.g., enjoyment, pleasure, happiness) over her negatively valenced experience (e.g., suffering, pain). "[W]hat is good for any individual is the enjoyable experience in her life, what is bad is the suffering in that life, and the life best for an individual is that with the greatest balance of enjoyment over suffering" (Crisp 2006, 622). Hedonism is an explanatory theory. It explains why Fabiola's close relationships or her professional success contribute to her well-being: They bring about a favorable hedonic balance of enjoyment over suffering.

1.1. Hedonism and the Inclusive Approach

Some philosophers defend hedonism on the grounds that it captures very well their commonsense judgments about well-being (Crisp 2006, Mendola 2006). And so hedonism is a live option. The network theory makes sense of philosophers' conventional wisdom about hedonism and so it too is a live option. And while the network theory provides us with a clear framework for organizing and making sense of the science, hedonism is bedeviled by both the fitting and privileging problems.

1.2. The Network Theory Is a Live Option

Hedonism and the network theory yield a considerable amount of overlap in their judgments about people's well-being. PCNs typically consist of states with a robustly favorable hedonic balance of enjoyment over suffering. And so for the network theory, people with more well-being will tend to have more (net) positive experiences. But the theories differ in their explanations.

Suppose Fabiola begins a meditation regimen that bolsters her well-being. The hedonist explains this in terms of her now having more net pleasure than she did before. For the network theory, the new regimen promotes her well-being because it brings about stable changes to Fabiola's life that strengthen her PCN. Perhaps some states that comprise her PCN change in intensity in ways that increase the robustness of her PCN. She is a bit less obsessed with work, which permits her to appreciate other successful aspects of her life, and she is a bit more patient with family and friends, which strengthens her close relationships. Or perhaps her PCN has grown to include more new causal drivers. She is now more at peace with her place in life and more optimistic about the future, which leads her to form new friendships and rekindle old ones. These changes make Fabiola's PCN more robust. It is now more resilient to life's occasional knocks.

For the network theory, the hedonic zing Fabiola receives from the new activity is part of the story of her increased well-being. But only a part. The network theory unearths and makes explicit the causal structure and dynamics of well-being, and it explains well-being in terms of factors that are causally implicated in its perpetuation. The explanation offered by the hedonist is on the right track but inevitably partial. *It ignores the causal structure of well-being, its stability and dynamics, and instead focuses exclusively on one part of that structure.* The hedonic tone of a person's life is typically a good indicator of the strength of the positive networks that make up her well-being. And so hedonism is a reasonable approximation of the truth about the nature of well-being. But it is not the whole truth.

This diagnosis of the problem with hedonism coheres nicely with what is probably the most serious objection to it. The objection begins with Nozick's experience machine thought experiment.

Suppose there were an experience machine that would give you any experience you desired. Superduper neuropsychologists could stimulate your brain so that you would think and feel you were writing a great novel, or making a friend, or reading an interesting book. All the time you would be floating in a tank, with electrodes attached to your brain. . . . Would you plug in? (Nozick 1974, 42–43).

We can sharpen the example by supposing that Richard and Anthony have exactly the same experiences, mostly positive, except that Richard is hooked up to the experience machine while Anthony is genuinely engaged with the world. According to hedonism, and any mental state view (any view that takes a person's well-being to be entirely a function of her mental states), the experience machine doesn't matter to a person's level of well-being. As long as Richard and Anthony are having exactly the same experiences and exactly the same mental states, hedonism implies that they have exactly the same levels of well-being. And as Roger Crisp notes, the conventional wisdom among philosophers is that this is wrong.

> Hedonism has a distinguished philosophical history. . . . In the twentieth century, however, hedonism became significantly less popular . . . [W]hile hedonism was down, Robert Nozick dealt it a near-fatal blow with his famous example of the experience machine. The result has been that these days hedonism receives little philosophical attention, and students are warned off it early on in their studies, often with a reference to Nozick (Crisp 2006, 619–620).

Most philosophers judge that Anthony has a higher level of well-being than Richard. And the network theory agrees.

I agree this is wrong!

The experience machine is a dramatic instance of a more general worry philosophers have about mental state theories: The quality of a person's experiences, or mental states more generally, might be inappropriate to the facts of her life. James Griffin makes the point nicely.

> I prefer, in important areas of my life, bitter truth to comfortable delusion. Even if I were surrounded by consummate actors able to give me sweet simulacra of love and affection, I should prefer the relatively bitter diet of their authentic reactions. And I should prefer it not because it would be morally better, or aesthetically better, or more noble, but because it would make for a better life for me to live (Griffin 1986, 9).

So suppose Don and Ed have exactly the same hedonic experiences, but Don's friends and family genuinely care for him, whereas Ed's friends and family only pretend to care for him— they actually don't like him at all (Kraut 1979, 177, Kagan 1998, 34–36). The conventional wisdom among philosophers is that Don has more well-being than Ed. Once again, the network theory agrees. The quality of our experience is not all there is to well-being.

For the network theory, hedonism is right to emphasize positive hedonic experience, but it is wrong to ignore other facets of PCNs—positive traits, positive attitudes, and successful interaction with the world. This diagnosis of what's wrong with hedonism accords nicely with Nozick's.

> What does matter to us in addition to our experiences? First, we want to do certain things, and not just have the experience of doing them. In the case of certain experiences, it is only because first we want to do the actions that we

want the experiences of doing them or thinking we've done them (1974, 43).

The network theory embraces the idea that a person's well-being involves her successful engagement with the world. Nozick continues.

> A second reason for not plugging in is that we want to be a certain way, to be a certain sort of person. Someone floating in a tank is an indeterminate blob. There is no answer to the question of what a person is like who has long been in the tank. Is he courageous, kind, intelligent, witty, loving? It's not merely that it's difficult to tell; there's no way he is (1974, 43).

Once again, the network theory is in harmony with Nozick's diagnosis. Having a high degree of well-being involves having certain attitudes and traits. Nozick offers one more reason for not plugging in.

> Thirdly, plugging into an experience machine limits us to a man-made reality, to a world no deeper or more important than that which people can construct. There is no actual contact with any deeper reality, though the experience of it can be simulated. Many persons desire to leave themselves open to such contact and to a plumbing of deeper significance (1974, 43).

I am unclear about what sort of "deeper reality" Nozick has in mind but a footnote suggests it involves religious or spiritual matters. If the point is that certain sorts of religious practices might be crucial to some people's well-being, the network theory can explain this. PCNs can be made up of many different causal nodes, after all, and some will include religious or spiritual practices and commitments as nodes.

Hedonism might have fared better had we started with the commonsense judgments of ordinary folk rather than philosophers. Felipe De Brigard argues that most people's intuitive reaction to the experience machine is not the result of their taking contact with reality to be an important prudential value (2010). Let's assume for the sake of argument that hedonism captures most non-philosophers' commonsense judgments about the experience machine better than the network theory. From the perspective of the inclusive approach, this would make little difference to their relative merits. Neither theory deviates from the commonsense evidence drastically enough to be defeated by it. Both are live options. So why do I spill so much ink on the commonsense evidence if it cannot, by itself, confirm or disconfirm any of the theories under consideration? My (not so) hidden agenda is to soften up the reader—to prepare you to accept the cost of giving up some of your firmly held intuitions for the benefits of a theory that best explains the evidence. Unless we are willing to surrender some of our commonsense judgments, the philosophical study of well-being is doomed to deadlock, Balkanization, and ultimately irrelevance.

1.3. Hedonism and Positive Psychology

Hedonism has great potential to organize and unify Positive Psychology, which is up to its ears in studies that measure positively and negatively valenced experience. This embarrassment of riches is, in fact, the source of the fitting problem for hedonism. As long as we are vague about what pleasure is, it is plausible to suppose that it is ubiquitous in the science. The fitting problem arises as soon as the hedonist tries to get specific.

First, the hedonist must choose a theory of pleasure (or happiness, enjoyment, etc.). Is it a basic, undefinable positive quality of experience? Or is it some positive cognitive attitude, like a desire or preference, toward an experience? Or is it something else? Next, the hedonist must fit that account of pleasure to the psychological literature. And there's the rub. Psychologists use many different instruments that, from an intuitive perspective, plausibly measure positive affect (or net positive affect). But these instruments measure states with different causal and correlational profiles. Which does the hedonist take to be central to Positive Psychology? Consider the recent controversy about whether income above the poverty line correlates with well-being (Easterlin 1973, 1995, Cummins 2000, Stevenson and Wolfers 2008, Leonhardt 2008). Kahneman and Deaton (2010) have tried to resolve this controversy by arguing that above the poverty line, *emotional well-being* (measured by questions about the frequency and intensity of positive and negative emotional experiences) does not correlate with income, but *life satisfaction* (measured on a scale with zero representing the worst possible life for the person and 10 the best) does correlate with (the logarithm of) income. Assume for the sake of argument that this is right. Instruments that measure life satisfaction tap a different state than instruments that measure emotional well-being. The hedonist needs to decide which one tracks pleasure. The hedonist has three potential answers: Neither is a plausible measure of pleasure, only one measures pleasure, or both do.

The best way for the hedonist to respond to the fitting problem is to adopt an expansive view of pleasure: Many instruments, including the life satisfaction and the emotional well-being instruments, measure different aspects of pleasure. The more restrictive options, the options that rule out life satisfaction or emotional well-being or both as reasonable measures of pleasure, make trouble for the hedonist. Consider the two claims under review:

1. Life satisfaction correlates with income.
2. Emotional well-being does not correlate with income.

The restrictive options imply that one or both of these claims is irrelevant to well-being. This violates common sense, or at least my common sense. This is not, given the inclusive approach, a serious strike against hedonism. The more serious problem is that the restrictive options force the hedonist to admit that Positive Psychology is more than the study of pleasure. It is also about whatever states are measured by the disfavored instrument or instruments (life satisfaction, emotional well-being or both). A restrictive hedonism cannot organize and make sense of the science as well as the network theory.

The expansive view of pleasure gives the hedonist the best chance of explaining Positive Psychology as the study of positively and negatively valenced experience. This form of hedonism, however, still faces the privileging problem. Positive Psychology studies many states besides positive and negative experiences. Why suppose that it is primarily about such experiences rather than various attitudes, character traits, or successful interactions with the world? The expansive hedonist has a plausible reply: All these other states are causally related to positively (and negatively) valenced experiences. But this claim, by itself, isn't enough to avoid the privileging problem. Positive Psychology studies rich causal networks involving positive experiences, emotions, attitudes, traits, and accomplishments. So it's not just positive experience that has these rich causal connections. On what grounds does the hedonist privilege the positive (and negative) experiences over all the rest? Why not suppose that Positive Psychology is primarily the study of positive traits or virtues? Or how to achieve success in various domains of life? In absence of a good argument for privileging pleasure as the correct lens through which to understand the psychological literature, it is more plausible to suppose that the psychology of well-being is the study of the structure and dynamics of PCNs. After all, such networks can be made up of all these sorts of states.

The expansive hedonist has another arrow in her quiver: What if pleasure, widely construed, is crucial to the dynamics of positive causal networks? Perhaps PCNs are best understood within a framework of *dynamic hedonism*: the main causal driver of PCNs, what explains the establishment and maintenance of PCNs, is (net) positively valenced experience. On this view, the network theory is transitional. Positive Psychology *is* the study of PCNs. But since PCNs are best understood in terms of dynamic hedonism, Positive Psychology is best understood to be the study of the causal dynamics of positive and negative experience.

The expansive hedonist might be right. Someone someday might give a coherent treatment of hedonic dynamics that unifies and makes sense of Positive Psychology. But right now, this is a promissory note. Another possibility is that the hedonist's very broad category of pleasure will fragment. Perhaps it is like the category *animals of Ecuador*. It consists of subcategories that are scientifically powerful and important—the poison tree frog, *Oophaga sylvatica*, for example, is fascinating for biological and social reasons. But the category *animals of Ecuador* (or, to pursue the analogy, *pleasure*) is not a theoretically or explanatorily perspicacious one.

One reason to think the expansive category will fragment is that different instruments that plausibly measure pleasure, broadly construed, seem to identify states with different causal and correlational profiles. We have already seen this with respect to life satisfaction and emotional well-being, which have different relationships to income. Now add to the list other pleasures that seem to have dissimilar causal profiles: Orgasms, eating chocolate, being amused or entertained or moved by a piece of art, the joy of success, the pride of accomplishment, being mindfully engrossed in a challenging problem, the gratification of volunteering at a food bank, the satisfaction with a life well lived, feeling optimistic or cheerful, and the countless other kinds of pleasures we are capable of experiencing—their causal profiles, their standard patterns of causes and effects, are sure to be extremely diverse.

Another reason to think pleasure will fragment is that the set of experiences that count as pleasant are heterogeneous. They feel different. There does not appear to be a common or essential intrinsic quality in every pleasure we are capable of experiencing. The heterogeneity objection to hedonism can only take us so far. There may be some way to unify these variegated experiences under a single theoretical umbrella (e.g., Crisp 2006). The dynamic hedonist might find some comfort in the neuroscience of pleasure. In the 1950s, scientists placed electrodes in the brains of rats that the rats could stimulate by pressing a bar. The rats would press a bar thousands of times an hour when electrodes stimulated certain parts of their brains (Olds 1956). This was taken to be evidence of a "pleasure center" in the brain (Heath 1972). The current view seems to be that there are two distinct neurochemical systems, one involving motivation (desire, craving, addiction) and the other involving pleasure (positive hedonic tone) and what earlier scientists thought were pleasure centers were probably more like addiction centers. The parts of the brain responsible for pleasure seem to involve "hedonic hotspots" that "when stimulated, amplify the sensation of pleasure—for example, making sweet things even more enjoyable" (Kringelbach and Berridge 2012, 45). Some neuroscientists have speculated that these hedonic hotspots are essential to pleasant experience, in all its phenomenological diversity.

The sensory pleasure of a delicious-tasting food feels different from pleasures of sex or drugs. Even more different seem social or cognitive pleasures of seeing a loved one or listening to music. But does each psychological pleasure have its own neural circuit? Perhaps not. Instead there appears heavy overlap, with a shared mesocorticolimbic circuit or single common neural currency, involved in all those diverse pleasures (Berridge and Kringelbach 2013, 295).

Perhaps neural hedonic hotspots should give hope to the expansive hedonist looking to explain Positive Psychology. But trying to make sense of the rich and varied PCNs that psychologists study, armed only with neural hotspots, seems to me a large and difficult job.

Perhaps someday someone will show how dynamic hedonism organizes and unifies Positive Psychology and in fact does so better than the network theory. But it seems at least as plausible to suppose that hedonism's broad central category, pleasure, will fragment into many different and interesting categories, in which case the narrower, individual pleasures will take their place alongside many other states (various attitudes, traits, and accomplishments) as important constituents of positive causal networks. Until dynamic hedonism develops a clear framework for understanding Positive Psychology, the network theory better explains the evidence.

2. Informed Desire Theory

Desire theories hold that a person is better off insofar as she gets what she wants, or more precisely, insofar as her desires are satisfied. A desire is satisfied when the content of the desire comes about, regardless of whether its coming about influences the

Some might argue or oppose

person's life. My desire that my child learn to swim is satisfied by his learning to swim, even if I get no pleasure from it and even if I have no idea whether he has learned to swim. For desire theories, not all desires are created equal. Some desires (e.g., that my children are healthy) are more important to my well-being than others (e.g., that my favorite sports team win the big game). James Griffin argues that the strength of a desire is not a matter of intensity or motivational force. My most intense desire might be to smoke or overeat, even though satisfaction of that desire might not increase my well-being. "[T]he relevant sense of 'strength' has to be, not motivational force, but rank in a cool preference ordering, an ordering that reflects appreciation of the nature of the objects of desire" (Griffin 1986, 15).

✗   The satisfaction of desires based on ignorance or misinformation can undermine well-being. Satisfying my desire to eat the delicious-looking banana split or to take the euphoria-inducing drug might undermine my well-being because the banana split is tainted and because the drug leads to addiction and ruin. Such desires would not have survived had I been appropriately informed and had I used that information in a rational way. This is why most desire theories hold that well-being involves only the satisfaction of *informed* desires. The best view of what is it for a desire to be informed is Peter Railton's notion of an individual's "objectified subjective interest."

> Give to an actual individual *A* unqualified cognitive and imaginative powers, and full factual and nomological information about his physical and psychological constitution, capacities, circumstances, history, and so on. *A* will have become *A*+, who has complete and vivid knowledge of himself and his environment, and whose instrumental rationality is in no way defective. We now ask *A*+ to tell us not what he currently wants, but what he would want his nonidealized

self *A* to want—or, more generally, to seek—were he to find himself in the actual condition and circumstances of *A*. . . . [W]e may assume there to be a reduction basis for his objectified subjective interests, namely, those facts about *A* and his circumstances that *A+* would combine with his general knowledge in arriving at his views about what he would want to want were he to step into *A*'s shoes (2003, 11).

So my informed desires are those desires my idealized self would want me (the non-idealized me) to want were he in my shoes.

2.1. The Informed Desire Theory and the Inclusive Approach

The informed desire theory captures the commonsense judgments of some philosophers very well and so it is a live option. The case against it is a comparative one. The network theory explains the entirety of the evidence better than the informed desire theory. The first step is to show that the network theory is also a live option because it explains conventional philosophical wisdom about the informed desire theory, both why it is intuitively powerful and why it is mistaken. The second step is to argue that the informed desire theory is not able to organize and explain Positive Psychology as well as the network theory. In particular, it faces a virulent form of the fitting problem.

2.2. The Network Theory Is a Live Option

Healthy people with a modicum of insight about themselves and how the world works tend to have desires that, if satisfied, would usually strengthen their PCNs. We want our relationships to be strong, we want our families to prosper, we want to be good to our friends and we want our friends to be good to us, we want to be happy, healthy, safe, and productive. These general desires engender particular desires that can vary widely given different people's situations. You want to buy that car and I want to sell it. So there is bound to be overlap in the judgments made by the network theory and desire theories. This overlap increases when we restrict ourselves to informed desire theories.

Received wisdom among philosophers is that a fundamental problem with informed desire theories is that the connection between well-being and informed desire satisfaction is not perfect. The satisfaction of at least some remote desires (desires whose satisfaction makes no difference to our experience) does not improve a person's well-being. Sandra's desire for posthumous fame or for there to be a prime number of atoms in the universe might survive full information. But my commonsense judgment says that whether or not these desires are satisfied is irrelevant to her well-being (Parfit 1984, Griffin 1986, Kagan 1998). Satisfaction of Jacques's informed desire to count the blades of grass on the college green might actually undermine his well-being (Rawls 1971, 432). The network theory takes these objections to be true. The satisfaction of Sandra's remote desires does nothing for her PCN, while the satisfaction of Jacques's grass counting desire might undermine his well-being by interrupting the smooth operation of his PCN. And indeed, proponents of informed desire theories have developed various fixes to try to account for their pretheoretic judgments—from permissive theories that count the satisfaction of all remote desires as relevant to well-being to strict theories that count no remote desires as relevant to well-being (e.g., Brandt 1979, Overvold 1982, Griffin 1986, Kavka 1986, Portmore 2007, Mendola 2009, Lukas 2010).

Another strike against informed desire theories is the explanatory direction problem: They confuse the nature of well-being with a reliable indicator of it. A perfectly reliable thermometer that reads 72 degrees does not make the ambient temperature 72 degrees. The ambient temperature—what it is—is the mean kinetic energy of the air molecules in the room. The thermometer merely reflects this deeper fact. This "nature vs. reliable indicator" objection has a long history in philosophy. In the *Euthyphro*, Socrates famously asks: "Is the pious loved by the gods because it is pious? Or is it pious because it is loved by the gods?" Plato's line of argument suggests we are to conclude that the explanation for why the gods love the good is that it is good, not the other way around. In the same way, what makes a strong friendship promote Joe's well-being is not that he desires it; rather, the strong friendship makes Joe's life better and as a result Joe desires it. According to the network theory, this intuitively compelling criticism of the informed desire theory is true. A strong friendship is to be desired for many reasons, perhaps even because it makes one's life better. But if a strong friendship contributes to Joe's well-being, it does so by establishing or strengthening his PCN or PCN fragments.

2.3. Informed Desire Theories and Positive Psychology

Both the network and the informed desire theories are live options. The reason to prefer the network theory is that it provides a superior framework for understanding the scientific evidence. Informed desire theories suffer from a severe fitting problem. Positive Psychology puts almost no effort into measuring desire satisfaction. Recall that desire satisfaction is an objective fact about the world. If I desire D, whether this desire has been satisfied depends on whether D is true or not. It is not a fact about whether I think it's been satisfied or whether I am satisfied with my life. If I have a strong informed desire to visit the Galapagos, Positive Psychology is not much interested in whether I've *actually visited* the Galapagos. It investigates whether I'm satisfied with my life, my work, my relationships; it investigates whether I believe I've gotten most of the important things I want in life; it tries to determine whether I usually have positive experiences; and it aims to identify my character strengths. In other words, Positive Psychology traffics in the central posits of hedonism (positive and negative experiences), the network theory (positive causal networks), and Aristotelianism (character strengths and virtues). But it is unconcerned with whether a person's idiosyncratic desires have been satisfied.

The fitting problem is especially serious for *informed* desire theories. Informed desires are idealizations. My informed desires are the desires I *would* have for myself if I were *far* more knowledgeable about myself and the world than I am, *far* more imaginative than I am, and *far* more instrumentally rational than I am. The problem is not that informed desires are always unknowable. They're not. We often identify a gap between a person's actual desires and informed desires. We frustrate the desire of the child to stick a fork in an electrical socket and we teach him not to do it; we hide the keys of our inebriated friend who wants to ride her motorcycle home after the party. We intervene paternalistically on the grounds of what we reasonably think the person would want, were he competent and informed. And our views on these matters are often true and justified. So the problem for informed desire theories is not that informed desires are unknowable. The problem is that Positive Psychology just doesn't care much about whether they have been satisfied.

The proponent of the informed desire theory has two replies to this worry. The first is to argue that psychologists measure desire satisfaction *indirectly*. Instruments that ask whether a person has gotten most of the important things she wants in life or whether she is satisfied with her life are reasonable measures of desire satisfaction, perhaps even of informed desire satisfaction. Like hedonism, the informed desire theory now faces the problem of an embarrassment of riches. There are *many* instruments that might be plausible indirect measures of desire satisfaction. But these instruments measure states that tend to have somewhat different causal profiles. And so the informed desire theorist needs to make some decisions. For example, which is a better measure of desire satisfaction, life-satisfaction instruments or emotional well-being instruments? And once a decision is made, the informed desire theorist will be faced with the privileging problem: Why suppose the state measured by that instrument is more important to understanding Positive Psychology than the scores of other states psychologists investigate? In absence of a solution to this problem, it is reasonable to assume the network theory better explains the scientific evidence.

The second reply to the worry that Positive Psychology seems uninterested in determining whether someone's informed desires have been fulfilled is to grant the point. Informed desires are idealizations. Science traffics in idealizations all the time. Physicists appeal to frictionless planes, and economists speculate about utility maximizing agents even though these things do not exist. And so there is nothing untoward about understanding Positive Psychology in terms of an idealization, namely, informed desires. Especially since, as we have already noted, we appeal to them all the time when we intervene paternalistically in a person's life by identifying a gap between what he *does* want and what he *should* want.

The problem with this reply is that while it's true that idealizations often appear in science, they tend to be *predictive and explanatory tools*, and Positive Psychology does not appeal to informed desires in its explanations or predictions. Within the framework of Newtonian mechanics, we assume gravity is the only force operating on a projectile to predict its motion; or we assume a block slides down a frictionless plane to calculate its velocity or acceleration. Within the framework of classical microeconomics, we assume buyers are utility maximizers to predict the marginal rate of substitution of two products. In these examples, scientists are making a prediction about a measurable quantity; and that prediction is derived by assuming that some part of the world behaves in an unrealistic fashion. Because of this idealization, we recognize that the prediction might be somewhat inaccurate. Because we ignore air resistance, for example, we do not expect the canon ball to travel in a perfect parabola. The proponent of the informed desire theory needs to show that her favored idealized posit, the informed desire, is a useful tool for predicting or explaining the empirical findings of Positive Psychology. And I see no plausible way to do this.

Informed desire theories do not appear to have a solution to the fitting problem. Their central construct is not something the science of well-being studies. Without a solution to the fitting problem, informed desire theories are not going to be able to explain the scientific evidence at all. And so they will not provide a better explanation of the evidence than the network theory.

3. Authentic Happiness

Compared to the network theory's other competitors, the authentic happiness view of well-being is young. Its most complete articulation is found in L. W. Sumner's *Welfare, Happiness, and Ethics* (1996). It is worth noting, given the inclusive approach, that some defenders of the authentic happiness view argue that its smooth fit with the science of well-being is a point in its favor (Tiberius 2006, 498). Sumner's view is deceptively simple: Well-being is happiness that is authentic. The form of happiness Sumner takes to be essential to well-being is *being happy or having a happy life*, which involves having a positive attitude toward your life or to some significant aspect of your life. This positive attitude must include both a cognitive and an affective component. The former is a positive evaluation of your life—from your perspective, given your standards, values, and expectations, you believe that your life is going well. The affective component involves a feeling of satisfaction or fulfillment, a sense that your life is rewarding. A young child or a dog might be happy in this affective sense without being happy in the cognitive sense. They can feel satisfied or fulfilled without having the cognitive capacity to judge their lives against some standard (Sumner 1996, 145–146).

The form of happiness Sumner takes to be crucial to well-being is fairly specialized, and we should distinguish it from other forms of happiness. Sumner identifies three kinds of happiness not equivalent to *being happy*. The first is *being happy with something or about something*. For example, you might be happy with your new car or about the recent election. This means you have a positive attitude toward your car or the election, even though you might not have a positive feeling of any kind. Second is *feeling happy*, which is being in a cheerful, upbeat mood. It is unlike *being happy about something* because it is generalized, it might not have a particular object, and because it always involves a feeling of good cheer or optimism. Hopefully you know this feeling—"No, I'm not happy about anything. I just feel happy!"—although it will sometimes annoy those burdened with a darker mood. And third is *having a happy disposition or personality*. This is a settled tendency to feel happy, or perhaps it is a personality trait that disposes one to usually have a mood of good cheer or optimism.

Suppose you are happy. You feel a sense of satisfaction and fulfillment about your life and upon reflection you judge your life positively according to your own standards. But what if your positive attitudes are the result of your standards having been warped by a situation that is oppressive, abusive or deprived? This is known as the problem of adaptive preferences. If your life evaluations are positive because your environment makes you feel unworthy of good things or just lucky not to be worse off, Sumner is forced to admit that you are happy. But he argues that your happiness is not authentic. And since well-being is authentic happiness, you do not have well-being. To be authentic, the evaluations that make up your happiness must be autonomous. They must have been freely chosen and not foisted upon you by a cruel, severe, or oppressive environment.

Suppose, again, that you are happy. What's more, the positive attitudes that make up your happiness were autonomously produced. Even so, what if your positive attitudes are based on false information, such that if you knew the truth, your attitudes would no longer be positive? Once again, Sumner is forced to admit that you are happy but perhaps not authentically happy. To be authentic, the judgments that make up a person's happiness must be both autonomous and *suitably informed*. How well informed must an autonomous person be in order for her life evaluations to be authentic? According to Sumner, "The place to start is with a (slightly) different question: when is (more) information relevant? The obvious answer, on a subjective account, is: whenever it would make a difference to a subject's affective response to her life, given her priorities" (1996, 160). A natural way to interpret Sumner here is to suppose that the evaluations that fix authentic happiness must be based on full and accurate information—and the agent is free to ignore whatever information would not make a difference to her "affective response to her life, given her priorities." Ultimately, I think this is the best and most plausible way to interpret the authentic happiness view, but Sumner explicitly rejects it.

For Sumner, the "reality requirement" at minimum rules out misinformation (Sumner 2000, 16). It's not clear whether he thinks it also requires full information, but I will assume that it does. Sumner rejects the reality requirement because he thinks it is possible for illusion-based happiness to count as authentic, and hence well-being.

> In my younger days I derived much comfort from the conviction that the course of my life, and of the world as a whole, was being directed by a benevolent deity. *When I could no longer sustain this illusion* I did not disavow the earlier comfort I derived from it; it got me through a difficult period of my life. When we reassess our lives in retrospect, and *from a superior vantage point*, there is no right answer to the question of what our reaction should be—that is surely up to us. Because a reality requirement stipulates a right answer—any happiness based on illusion can make no intrinsic contribution to our well-being—it must be rejected as presumptuously dogmatic (1996, 158–159, emphasis added).

This makes clear that authentic happiness, like informed desire, is an idealization. It requires that we evaluate our lives based on knowledge we might never actually have (for example, whether or not a benevolent deity directs our lives). Putting aside this worry, Sumner is not correct to suppose that the reality or full information requirement "stipulates a right answer." It only requires that one consider all information (or perhaps just no misinformation) in making an evaluation. One is free to consider or ignore any truths one chooses in coming up with "a right answer." I suspect that Sumner rejects the full information requirement because he does not distinguish two different questions.

1. If we keep fixed the facts of *A*'s happy life at time 1, was he *authentically* happy at time 1?

2. If we alter the facts of *A*'s life so that he were fully informed (or at least not misinformed) at time 1, would *A* have remained happy (and thus, assuming autonomy, authentically happy)?

The simplest and best way to interpret the authentic happiness view is to take the answer to (2) to also be the answer to (1). So if it would have been devastating for Sumner at time 1 to be fully informed (or not misinformed) about his religious beliefs, then he was not authentically happy at time 1. Sumner does not adopt this interpretation; otherwise he would have simply embraced the full information (or the reality) requirement. He seems to want to leave open the possibility that he was authentically happy at time 1 even though he would not have been happy had he learned the truth at that time. I don't see how Sumner can pull this off.

According to Sumner, a person's happiness—that is, the evaluations that constitute his happiness—is informed when he reassesses his life "in retrospect, and from a superior vantage point." This superior vantage point seems to involve full information ("When I could no longer sustain this illusion"). So I interpret Sumner's informational requirement to involve two stages.

1. *A*+ (the idealized, fully informed version of *A*) decides what information is relevant to *A*'s authentic happiness.
2. An appropriately informed evaluation of *A*'s life is the evaluation *A* would make on the basis of the information that *A*+ identified as relevant.

This would deliver the results Sumner wants. Even if some piece of information would devastate *A* and ruin his happiness, *A*+ might decide that that information is not relevant to *A*'s authentic happiness. And so *A* would not have access to that information in making an appropriately informed evaluation of his life.

If this interpretation is right, there is a serious gap in Sumner's theory: On what grounds is A+ supposed to decide whether a piece of information is relevant to A's authentic happiness? Ignoring circular views (which would have A+ take A's well-being into account), here are two possible answers.

1. Sumner says that relevant information is information that "would make a difference to a subject's affective response to her life, given her priorities" (1996, 160). But if A+ is supposed to take as relevant all information that would produce an "affective response" in A given A's priorities, this is equivalent to the full information requirement: Relevant information is all the information that would make a difference to A's actual evaluation.

2. Perhaps relevant information is information that would make a difference to *A-at-a-later-time*. In all of Sumner's examples, it is *A-at-a-later-time* whose judgments fix whether some piece of information is relevant to A's authentic happiness. It is Sumner, after he "could no longer sustain this illusion" concerning his religious views, who determines whether his previous self was authentically happy. In another example, A is happy in a relationship, but she does not know that her partner is "faithless and self-serving" (157). Upon being undeceived, Sumner argues that there is no requirement that she revise downward her life evaluation. Note the past tense: "We always have the alternative available of accepting the good times we *enjoyed* with little or no regret and then moving on with our lives" (158, emphasis added). If A was happy but deceived at time 1, that happiness would count as authentic if at a later time A is undeceived and still

positively evaluates her life at time 1. But if *A*'s informed evaluation at time 1 would have been different than her informed evaluation at time 2, there must be some difference (beyond the full information) between *A* at time 1 and *A* at time 2 to explain the changed evaluation. But Sumner does not explain what it is. Perhaps it is as simple as the perspective one acquires after a certain amount of time has passed. But perspectives change. At time 2, a fully informed *A* might evaluate his life at time 1 positively; but at an even later time, time 3, he might evaluate his life at time 1 negatively (Mendola 2006, 453). Does *A*'s well-being at time 1 change depending on *A*'s later informed evaluations? That seems deeply counterintuitive, and it is not an implication Sumner ever explicitly endorses.

Valerie Tiberius has suggested that perhaps the evaluations that constitute well-being are those that one comes to after wise reflection on one's values (2006, 2008). While I think this is a good move for the proponent of authentic happiness, the problem for the view comes much earlier. Any view that takes well-being to consist of life evaluations (whether actual or idealized) is not going to provide a useful way to organize and make sense of Positive Psychology. In what follows, I will consider a simple and natural version of the view, one that embraces the full information requirement. Problems with the simple view will generalize to more complex versions of the theory.

3.1. Authentic Happiness and the Inclusive Approach

The authentic happiness view is a live theory. It captures our commonsense judgments about well-being reasonably well. The two-step argument for the network theory and against this competitor should, by now, be familiar. The network theory is also a live option because it is able to explain both what is intuitively right and what is intuitively wrong about the authentic happiness view. The network theory is superior to the authentic happiness view because it does a better job explaining the scientific evidence.

3.2. The Network Theory Is a Live Option

There is bound to be considerable overlap in the well-being judgments rendered by the network theory and by the authentic happiness view. People with more robust PCNs will tend to evaluate their lives more positively. This is not an accident. The life of a person who has a robust PCN will be full of positive emotions, attitudes, traits, and accomplishments. And so she is likely to evaluate her life positively. This accounts for the intuitive pull of the authentic happiness view. The fundamental problem with authentic happiness views is that life evaluations are, at best, reliable indicators of well-being. They are not what well-being is. Any evaluation I make of how well my life is going, if all goes well, *accurately represents* my level of well-being. The authentic happiness view, like the informed desire theory, confuses what well-being is with a reliable indicator of well-being. One way to appreciate the force of this objection is to consider again the fundamental challenge facing authentic happiness views: to identify the appropriate perspective from which one should make life evaluations (Haybron 2008). For my life evaluation to reflect my well-being, do I have to be fully autonomous, fully informed, wise? What makes one perspective more appropriate than another? I submit that the proponent of the authentic happiness view is trying to identify the perspective that puts a person in position to make consistently accurate judgments about her own well-being. The right perspective is the one from which a person's life evaluations *accurately represent* the strength of her PCN and PCN fragments.

3.3. Authentic Happiness and Positive Psychology

Valerie Tiberius has argued that theories of well-being should cohere with the empirical literature on well-being; and so an advantage of the authentic happiness view is that the empirical literature is riddled with life evaluations of the kind Sumner takes to be constitutive of happiness. "[T]he life-satisfaction program in psychology is robust and productive. Life-Satisfaction research is still in its early stages, but there is good evidence that life-satisfaction can be measured, that it correlates well with other intuitively compelling values, and that there are things we can do to increase it in ourselves and others" (2006, 498). Tiberius is right that Positive Psychology focuses considerable attention on life-satisfaction measures. But in making sense of a body of empirical research, we must distinguish the discipline's objects of study from the instruments it uses to measure those objects. Telescopes are tools for studying the heavens, and it is important for astronomy to have accurate, well-calibrated tools. But despite the centrality of telescopes to the study of astronomy, astronomy is not the study of telescopes. Similarly, first-person evaluations of the sort taken to be important by authentic happiness views are vital tools psychologists use to study well-being. And so whether these tools are accurate and reliable and how to make them more accurate and reliable are central issues to the empirical study of well-being (Angner 2010, Haybron 2011a). But it is a mistake to suppose that Positive Psychology is the study of how people evaluate their lives. Debates about authentic happiness are properly understood to be debates about the conditions under which self-reports are accurate indicators of well-being. Sumner argues that self-reports are accurate when they are informed and autonomous. Tiberius adds that self-reports are more accurate after one has reflected wisely on one's values. These claims are very plausible. But they are claims about how to measure well-being. They are not claims about the nature of well-being.

4. Aristotelian Theories of Well-Being

While there is some question about whether Aristotle's notion of *eudaimonia* is best understood as *well-being*, a number of contemporary philosophers have defended eudaimonic views of well-being explicitly inspired by Aristotle (e.g., Foot 2002, Hursthouse 2002, Kraut 2007). And so it is reasonable to consider Aristotelian theories as an alternative to the network theory. The gist of the Aristotelian view is attractive: Well-being involves a robust, active engagement with the world that springs from a virtuous character and that is naturally adorned with various kinds of success. What's more, the virtuous person naturally takes pleasure in acting virtuously: "[T]he pleasures of those who are fond of noble things are pleasant by nature. Actions in accordance with virtue are like this, so that they are pleasant to these people as well as in themselves. Their life therefore has no need of pleasure as some kind of lucky ornament, but contains its pleasure in itself." Or more concisely, "actions in accordance with virtue are pleasant in themselves" (Aristotle 2000, 1099a).

4.1. Aristotelian Theories and the Inclusive Approach

There is a close affinity between Aristotle's theory and the network theory. Both are live options. Despite their similarities, an Aristotelian once told me that he could never accept the network theory because it allows for the possibility that the wicked might have a high degree of well-being. In cases of implacably opposed commonsense well-being judgments, the inclusive approach asks us to choose the theory that best explains the entirety of the evidence. That, I will argue, is the network theory.

4.2. The Network Theory Is a Live Option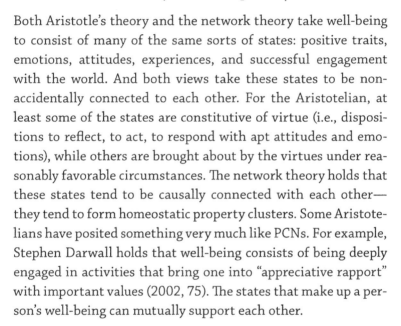

Both Aristotle's theory and the network theory take well-being to consist of many of the same sorts of states: positive traits, emotions, attitudes, experiences, and successful engagement with the world. And both views take these states to be non-accidentally connected to each other. For the Aristotelian, at least some of the states are constitutive of virtue (i.e., dispositions to reflect, to act, to respond with apt attitudes and emotions), while others are brought about by the virtues under reasonably favorable circumstances. The network theory holds that these states tend to be causally connected with each other—they tend to form homeostatic property clusters. Some Aristotelians have posited something very much like PCNs. For example, Stephen Darwall holds that well-being consists of being deeply engaged in activities that bring one into "appreciative rapport" with important values (2002, 75). The states that make up a person's well-being can mutually support each other.

> Because merit ramifies up and out, its appreciation ramifies up and out also. This means that the prudential value of an individual instance is likely to be substantially enhanced and supported by the prudential value of its branching offshoots. In this way, virtuous activity tends to create and partake of coherent structures of mutually supporting prudential value (102).

That sounds a lot like positive causal networks. Given the overlap between the theories and given that Aristotle's theory is a live option, the network theory is a live option as well.

To appreciate what is distinctive about Aristotelian views of well-being, consider a relatively weak view about the relationship between well-being and moral value. Let's call it the *normative consilience thesis*: Well-being is normally associated with moral virtue and goodness. We've seen evidence that there are causal connections between a life of well-being and a life of virtue, of value, and of good deeds. Many studies have shown a relationship between well-being and pro-social attitudes and behaviors. Happier people are more likely to do volunteer work; and volunteer work tends to make people happy. Positive affect makes people friendlier, more generous, more outgoing, and less likely to fall victim to the Own Race Bias. Moralized theories of well-being, such as Aristotle's, hold that normative consilience is not enough. A life of well-being *must* be a life consisting of significant positive moral value. For Aristotle's theory, virtue is essential to well-being. And so it judges that Josef, the thriving but wicked person from chapter 2, cannot have well-being. But for many other theories, including hedonism, informed desire theories, and the network theory, it is possible for the non-virtuous to have high degrees of well-being.

No clever example that shows Aristotle's theory getting my commonsense judgments wrong is going to convince the sophisticated Aristotelian that either her theory or her commonsense judgments are wrong. And really, why should it? The same point holds for the proponents of hedonism, informed desire theories, and all the rest. This is the problem with the traditional approach. It promises more centuries of stalemates, of ever more sophisticated theories that better capture the commonsense judgments of devotees of a particular philosophical outlook. The inclusive approach offers a way to break the dead-lock by asking theories to account for more than just our com-monsense judgments.

4.3. Moralized Views of Well-Being and Positive Psychology

Moralized accounts of well-being must presuppose some rea-sonably specific moral theory. For example, on Darwall's view, we need some account of the nature of agent-neutral values. (Such values for Darwall include more than just moral values.) And on Aristotle's view, we need some clear account of the virtues. If the moral theory is vague or incomplete, such im-perfections will infect the theory of well-being. Does the fact that one is a religious zealot or a sexual libertine undermine to at least some degree one's well-being? What if one is care-lessly wasteful with the Earth's resources, a seller of illegal but not especially harmful drugs, a carnivore, a corporate raider, or a negligent parent? The problem for the moralized theory can be framed in terms of a dilemma. Either the mor-alized theory of well-being passes clear judgments about these cases or it does not. If it does not, if it does not ascribe a well-being status to these people, then the theory cannot be applied to these cases. Such a radically incomplete theory is not going to capture either the commonsense or the scientific evidence better than its competitors. If the theory does pass clear judgments about these cases, the challenge is to explain how such discriminations help us to understand the empiri-cal literature. The worry here does not rest on any kind of skepticism about morality. Assume for the sake of argument that there are moral truths. The point is that it's not clear how such truths help us to make sense of the empirical dis-coveries made by psychologists who study happiness and well-being. Once we fix the non-moral facts about carnivores, it's hard to see how it would shed any light on what psychologists might discover about them to add that eating meat is morally wrong or morally permissible. To see this, let's focus on virtue.

A theory that takes virtue to be necessary for well-being needs an account of virtue. Aristotle defended a teleological view of nature, according to which natural objects have a purpose or function. He identified the highest human good with the distinctive function of humans. And that function is (roughly) the virtuous exercise of reason in guiding our lives. Contemporary Aristotelians have explained the virtues in various ways, usually in terms of some notion of flourishing (Foot 2002, Hursthouse 2002, Kraut 2007). While Aristotle's theory of virtue is canonical, it is not unchallenged. Any moral theory can explain the virtues as essentially nature's way of getting people to spontaneously do the right thing. A duty-based theory of morality might take virtue to be a strength of character that allows a person to do her duty (Kant 1964, 38). A utilitarian theory might take virtues to be character traits that tend to bring about positive consequences (Mill 1861/1969). What is distinctive about the Aristotelian approach is that it does not take some independent moral framework to be theoretically prior to its account of virtue.

Given these various accounts of virtue, we need to ask whether the Aristotelian view of the virtues helps us to understand Positive Psychology better than a duty-based or consequentialist view of the virtues. Of course, we also need to ask whether any of these moralized views of well-being make better sense of Positive Psychology than a non-moralized view like the network theory. To explore these questions, let's turn to a line of research that is the best hope for the Aristotelian. Psychologists Christopher Peterson and Martin Seligman have proposed an impressive classification scheme for virtues and character strengths (2004). If Aristotle's conception of the virtues is to help us understand the empirical literature, this is where it will work its magic. Peterson and Seligman identify six core virtues.

> Virtues are the core characteristics valued by moral philosophers and religious thinkers: wisdom, courage, humanity, justice, temperance, and transcendence. These six broad categories of virtue emerge consistently from historical surveys. . . . We argue that these are universal, perhaps grounded in biology through an evolutionary process that selected for these aspects of excellence as means of solving the important tasks necessary for survival of the species. We speculate that all these virtues must be present at above-threshold values for an individual to be deemed of good character (13).

Subsumed under each virtue is a set of character strengths, "the psychological ingredients—processes or mechanisms—that define the virtues. Said another way, they are distinguishable routes to displaying one or another of the virtues" (13). So, for example, character strengths that define the virtue of transcendence include gratitude, hope, humor, spirituality, and appreciation of beauty and excellence (30).

These character strengths are not derived from some Aristotelian view about the highest good or the distinctive function of humans. Nor are they derived from the moral theories of Kant or Mill. Peterson and Seligman arrived at their list by an inductive process. They began by casting a startlingly wide net: brainstorming with well-known scholars (such as Robert Nozick and George Vaillant), searching historical and contemporary texts that focus on virtues (works by Charlemagne, Benjamin Franklin, and William Bennett), and identifying "virtue-relevant messages in Hallmark greeting cards, bumper stickers, Saturday Evening Post covers by Norman Rockwell, personal ads, popular song lyrics, graffiti, Tarot cards, the profiles of Pokemon characters, and the residence halls of Hogwarts" (15). The authors winnowed their list with a set of 10 criteria they take to be typical of (though not essential to) a character strength (17–28). The list naturally breaks down into three distinct groups.

1. Three items are criteria for character traits: A character strength must be a reasonably robust trait (23), it can be manifested early in some people (prodigies) (25), and it can be totally lacking in others (26).
2. One item is a uniqueness criterion: A character strength must be distinct from and not reducible to other traits.
3. Six items are features standardly associated with traits that are positively valenced: They contribute to "fulfillments that constitute the good life" (17), are valued for their own sake (19), typically produce admiration in others (21), do not have opposite traits that can be described positively (22), are embodied in "consensual paragons" (24), and are often nurtured and supported by social institutions (27).

The authors then checked their proposed list of character strengths against various cultural and historical traditions (i.e., Confucian, Taoist, Buddhist, Hindu, Athenian, and Judeo-Christian virtues) as well as various psychological and philosophical studies of virtues and character strengths.

Given a traditional approach to the study of philosophy, the inductive procedure used by these psychologists to identify virtues will seem haphazard and theoretically crude. But from the perspective of the network theory, it was an effective method for discovering traits that promote well-being. The goal of the character strengths project is an empirical one: to provisionally identify traits that tend to play crucial roles in positive causal networks. And that is precisely what Peterson and Seligman do. The heart of their book consists of chapters that go into considerable detail on what we know about each character strength. Each chapter explains how the character strength is measured and the role it tends to play in various positive causal networks: its correlates and consequences, its typical development, its enabling and inhibiting factors, gender and cultural differences, and deliberate interventions that tend to promote it. In other words, each chapter spells out the ways in which character strengths are both cause and effect of positive emotions, attitudes, other traits, and various accomplishments. The network theory places this empirical project within a larger theoretical context: Positive Psychology is the study of PCNs, and the character strengths project involves studying traits that tend to be embedded in such networks. It smoothly makes sense of Positive Psychology and of the place of the character strength literature within it. Aristotle's theory does not approach this unifying power.

If we focus just on the character strength literature, Aristotle's theory should shine. But it doesn't. The character strengths identified by Peterson and Seligman can be intuitively understood to be virtues. But nothing in the empirical literature is illuminated by any *particular* view about the nature of the virtues. Positive Psychology studies traits that are important to establishing, maintaining, and strengthening positive causal networks. But the science is completely insensitive to whether or not these count as virtues, and if they do, whether they are best understood in the manner of Aristotle, Kant, Mill, or anyone else. To put this point another way: The empirical project of accounting for traits that are causally important in PCNs is consistent with a wide variety of moral perspectives and a wide variety of views about the nature of virtue.[1]

To sum up, the evidence of common sense leads to an impasse. Different philosophers have different intuitive judgments about whether the non-virtuous can have a high degree of well-being. To break this deadlock, the inclusive approach asks us to side with the theory that best explains the scientific evidence. I have argued that the network theory makes much better sense of Positive Psychology than does any moralized theory, including Aristotle's. The empirical effort to understand character strengths is an attempt to identify traits that typically appear in positive causal networks and to understand the role those traits tend to play in those networks. The attempt to impose a *particular* view about the nature of virtue on the empirical literature is not helpful in understanding, organizing, or making sense of that research. The totality of the evidence supports the network theory much better than it does Aristotle's theory or, in fact, any moralized theory of well-being.

5. Conclusion

The failure of traditional philosophical theories to fit smoothly with empirical research is not a new insight. In a recent article that has received considerable attention, the psychologists Todd Kashdan, Robert Biswas-Diener, and Laura King make exactly this point.

> Eudaimonia and hedonic happiness are intriguing philosophical concepts. We are skeptical, however, that they are

---

1. Given the firm divide between philosophy and science implicit in the traditional approach to the study of well-being, I suspect this is a conclusion most traditional philosophers will embrace.

the most useful way to frame contemporary research in well-being. While they are entirely appropriate to the philosophical traditions in which they were produced, these concepts do not translate well to modern scientific and empirical inquiry (2008, 227).

This chapter has been an extended argument for this thesis. The reason these theories do not sit comfortably with contemporary psychological research is that the "tradition in which [these theories] were produced" either predates scientific psychology or takes psychology to be irrelevant to uncovering the nature of well-being. Luminaries like Aristotle and Bentham had no choice but to rely only on their wisdom, experience, and common sense in developing their theories of well-being. The science of well-being did not exist in their day. The inclusive approach is motivated by the idea that we now have a wider array of evidence at our disposal—evidence that includes the large body of empirical research on well-being as well as the prescient insights and theoretical speculations of these great philosophers.

The case for the network theory is not that it captures the intuitions of the informed desire theorist better than the informed desire theory. It doesn't. It doesn't capture the hedonist's intuitions better than hedonism. And it doesn't capture the Aristotelian's intuitions better than Aristotle. The network theory doesn't even capture my own commonsense judgments perfectly. Arguing for a view of well-being *solely* on the grounds of common sense is a recipe for dissensus and deadlock. If I get to judge your theory in terms of whether it captures *my* commonsense judgments, then in the face of my settled insistence that your theory does not, nothing else you can say will move me. We are at an impasse. But if the main goal of your theory is to capture a wide range of evidence of which my commonsense judgments are but a small part, then in the face of my firm insistence that your theory doesn't capture all my judgments, you have a straightforward and compelling reply. You can rationally defeat my resistance by pointing to the fallibility of commonsense judgment and to the impressive explanatory power of your theory. Of course, I might insist upon the epistemic sublimity of my commonsense judgments and refuse to budge. But that would be my problem, not yours.

Chapter 6

Issues in the Psychology of Happiness and Well-Being

Theory and evidence are mutually reinforcing. Evidence shapes our theories. And our theories, if they are good ones, repay this debt by helping to clarify and resolve issues that arise in scientific practice. I have argued that the evidence supports the network theory. This chapter aims to show that the network theory can begin to repay this debt by helping to clarify and sometimes resolve open issues that arise in Positive Psychology.

1. The Placeholder View of Happiness

There is a puzzle about the way the network theory would have us understand Positive Psychology. If it really is the study of well-being, why do psychologists so often report their findings in terms of *happiness*? People who score high on certain measures are taken to be "very happy people" (Diener and Seligman 2002); a study on the habits of people instantiating PCNs is described in terms of "[t]he cognitive and motivational processes by which happy people are able to artfully sustain their happiness" (Abbe,

Tkach, and Lyubomirsky 2003, 385); a popular book about how we can flourish is called *The Happiness Hypothesis* (Haidt 2006); the finding that most people score in the positive range on a well-being scale is reported as "most people are happy" (Diener and Diener 1996); and when psychologists seek to use what they've learned to propose "empirical answers to philosophical questions" they pose those questions in terms of happiness (Kesebir and Diener 2008).

Should we understand Positive Psychology to be the study of happiness rather than well-being? For the network theory, the crucial point is that Positive Psychology is the study of positive causal networks. We can call them what we like. I will continue to use my preferred terminology because I think it best fits common sense. Even so, happiness is a central topic of study in Positive Psychology. There are many views about happiness to choose from. L. W. Sumner distinguishes four: being happy about something, being in a happy mood, having a happy personality, and being happy (1996, 143–147). Daniel Haybron distinguishes a descriptive psychological notion of happiness from a normative notion of happiness that is connected to well-being (2011b). And under the umbrella of psychological theories, Haybron distinguishes hedonist, life satisfaction, emotional state, and hybrid theories of happiness. Which of these senses of happiness are psychologists investigating? This is the wrong question.

The inclusive approach recommends we identify happiness with an item in the world psychologists investigate, philosophers theorize about, and laypeople refer to. Underwriting psychological practice is, I contend, the placeholder view of happiness. Happiness is *positive-states-of-mind-and-the-mechanisms-responsible-for-them-whatever-they-may-be*. The first part of the placeholder view, namely that happiness involves positive states of mind, has been defended by Daniel Haybron (2011b). A striking fact about psychological practice is that psychologists usually frame their results in terms of happiness in studies where they used a self-report instrument that asks about subjective states. These instruments typically ask people to report on their positive states of mind, which can include positive emotions (joy), states with a positive experiential "feel" (e.g., pleasure), or propositional attitudes involving positive attitudes (e.g., *excited* about the game, *optimistic* that we'll win), or positive propositions (e.g., thinking that *I have gotten most of the things I want in life*). But for the placeholder view, positive states of mind are only half the story. Psychologists also seek to understand the underlying states or mechanisms responsible for these positive states of mind.

The placeholder view fits neatly in the network theory framework. Positive Psychology is the study of positive causal networks. Positive states of mind are crucial to many of these networks. But we don't yet know much about how they work: What neurochemical mechanisms underlie them? How do they interact with negative states of mind? What role do they play in establishing or fostering PCNs? The placeholder view does not resolve any of these issues. They are for the scientists to decide. Rather, it places happiness within a framework that makes sense of psychological practice: Psychologists are proposing and testing hypotheses about positive states of mind, how they come about, their relationship to negative states of mind, and the broader role they play in our lives.

One might object to the placeholder view by insisting that happiness consists of the consciously available positive states of mind by themselves. The underlying mechanisms are not *part* of happiness. They are instead what brings about or causes happiness. While this suggestion might answer to many people's commonsense notion of happiness, the problem is that it artificially imports a form of dualism on psychological practice. Dualism holds that non-physical mental states are somehow the products of physical brain states. While dualism might be the view of common sense, it is not assumed in how psychologists go about studying happiness. That's not to say that no psychologist is a dualist. Rather, it is to say that psychological research is not committed from the beginning of inquiry to some form of dualism about happiness. In fact, it is best to understand psychology as undecided about the mechanisms responsible for happiness. The placeholder view recognizes this gap in our knowledge by being insistently vague.

It is common for psychology articles to begin with a menu of philosophical positions on happiness. And philosophers raise reasonable worries about whether the psychologist's tools are capable of reliably measuring a philosophically important state of happiness (Griffin 2007, Haybron 2007). The placeholder view gives the psychologist principled ways to answer these tough philosophical questions. It is common for scientists to study something without a clear idea of what it is. Scientists studied light for centuries even while they battled about whether it was made of particles or waves. It is also common for scientists to defer tough philosophical questions about what they're studying. When Newton was pressed about what gravity is, a force that seems to act at a distance as if by magic, he famously replied, "Hypothesis non fingo" (I frame no hypothesis). To the question "But what is happiness?" the placeholder view sanctions this kind of Newtonian demurral: "We don't know yet. That's what we're trying to find out!" And the correct response to the worry that psychologists are not measuring a philosophically important state of happiness is to simply grant the point: "That may be true. But we're not necessarily trying to measure a state that is central to some philosophical theory about happiness or well-being. We're trying to understand a pretty important real-world phenomenon." Psychologists studying happiness are not slowed down by philosophical worries. This is a reason to think that the placeholder view accurately describes the view of happiness implicit in psychological practice.

2. Subjective Well-Being

Psychologists use surveys that ask people to evaluate their lives. This research and the states investigated by it go under the umbrella term, Subjective Well-Being (SWB). The person most closely associated with this research, Ed Diener, has argued that SWB instruments involve three characteristic features: They measure people's subjective evaluations; they include positive measures of mental health; and they include a global, integrated evaluation of a person's life (1984, 543–544). SWB instruments are many and varied.[1] A popular measure is the five-item Satisfaction with Life Scale.

_____In most ways my life is close to my ideal.

_____The conditions of my life are excellent.

_____I am satisfied with my life.

_____So far I have gotten the important things I want in life.

_____If I could live my life over, I would change almost nothing.

Instructions for administering the scale are: Below are five statements that you may agree or disagree with. Using the 1–7

---

1. SWB surveys include single-item instruments (Cantril 1965, Gurin, Veroff, and Field 1960), multi-item instruments (Bradburn 1969, Campbell, Converse, and Rodgers 1976), instruments that ask about different domains of life (e.g., work, marriage), and different periods of time (e.g., the current moment, the last week, the last month). Experience sampling methods use beepers or cell phones to prompt people at random times of the day to evaluate their current states (Stone, Shiffman, and DeVries 1999). SWB instruments typically ask for evaluations of people's lives (or some portion of their lives), for a report on their affect, or both. For example, Cantril's Ladder is a single-item instrument that asks people to evaluate their lives, and the Gurin Scale is a single-item instrument that asks people whether they are (a) very happy, (b) pretty happy, or (c) not too happy.

scale below, indicate your agreement with each item by placing the appropriate number on the line preceding that item.
Please be open and honest in your responding. The 7-point
scale is: 1 = strongly disagree, 2 = disagree, 3 = slightly disagree, 4 = neither agree nor disagree, 5 = slightly agree, 6 =
agree, 7 = strongly agree (Diener et al. 1985, 72).

Another common instrument used by psychologists is PANAS. It
measures positive affect (PA) and negative affect (NA). It lists a
number of "feelings and emotions" (e.g., interested, upset, hos-
tile, enthusiastic, ashamed) and asks to what extent one has felt
this way over some recent period of time (Watson, Clark, and
Tellegen 1988).

In a wide-ranging review, Diener, Scollon, and Lucas argue that
SWB has a hierarchical structure. At the highest level is a "general
evaluation of a person's life." Below this level are four components
that are "moderately correlated" but "conceptually related." They
are positive affect, negative affect, satisfaction, and domain satisfaction. And "within each of these four components, there are
more fine-grained distinctions that can be made." These finer-
grained components include, but are not limited to, joy, contentment, happiness, and love under positive affect; sadness, anger,
worry, and stress under negative affect; life satisfaction, fulfillment, meaning, and success under satisfaction; work, marriage,
health, and leisure under domain satisfaction (2003, 192). Different SWB researchers tend to focus on different aspects of SWB
(191). This framework for understanding SWB, by capturing the
diversity and conceptual untidiness of Positive Psychology, makes
vivid the privileging problem: How can a theory of well-being organize and unify this discipline? The network theory does this by
taking Positive Psychology to be the study of positive causal networks. And many of the items Diener, Scollon, and Lucas take to
be part of SWB are often links in positive causal networks.

[handwritten marginal note: These all link to positive causal network]

Debates about SWB measures center on claims that they suffer from false positives (tapping into phenomena that have nothing to do with well-being) and from false negatives (failing to measure changes in well-being). In this section, I want to consider these objections and suggest that the network theory offers a useful framework for understanding these debates: Criticisms of SWB instruments are arguments for doubting that such instruments accurately represent facts about PCNs or PCN fragments; replies to these criticisms aim to show that SWB instruments do accurately represent such facts. In the following section, I will argue that although there are reasons to doubt that any single SWB instrument by itself always closely tracks well-being, there is no good reason for general skepticism about what we can learn from SWB instruments.

The first worry about SWB instruments is that they suffer from false positives—they are sensitive to factors they shouldn't be measuring. This worry begins with the fact that SWB judgments are context-sensitive. Many factors influence SWB judgments: the weather, lead-in questions (e.g., being asked about dating frequency or marital satisfaction), the presence of other people (e.g., a person of the opposite sex or a person with a physical disability), and the recollection of positive or negative events. Schwarz and Strack (1999) suggest that we make SWB judgments by identifying a target (some part of our lives that we are to evaluate) and a standard (some yardstick we use to judge the target) and then assessing that target using that standard. But this evaluative process can go awry in various ways. The weather and thoughts about our dating frequency can, unbeknownst to us, influence our view about the target of our evaluation. Psychologists know techniques to forestall these effects. For example, explicitly asking people about the weather eliminates weather effects. A factor that influences a person's SWB judgments is what she uses, often implicitly, as her comparison class. A person who consistently compares herself to people who are better off (upward comparison) is likely to report being less satisfied with her life than if she were to consistently compare herself to people who are similar (lateral comparison) or worse off (downward comparison). So being in the presence of someone who prompts us to make a downward comparison will tend to boost our SWB scores.

These findings raise the specter that SWB reports systematically fail to accurately represent facts about a person's well-being. They are largely manifestations of fleeting contextual factors—"transient influences"—rather than fundamental facts about how well our lives are going (Schwarz and Strack 1999, 79). But it gets worse. SWB reports are surprisingly insensitive to facts that many of us would deem to be fundamental to how well our lives are going.

The second worry about SWB instruments is that they suffer from false negatives—SWB reports don't track objective life circumstances that (the objection goes) reflect on our well-being. Age, education, income, having children, intelligence, physical attractiveness—these are all weakly correlated with SWB reports (Argyle 1999; Peterson 2006). A dramatic example of the insensitivity of SWB measures to objective life circumstances is Biswas-Diener and Diener's (2001) study of slum dwellers, prostitutes, and homeless people in Calcutta, India. Participants live in "extremely adverse conditions . . . suffer from poor health and sanitation, live in crowded conditions, and occupy dwellings of poor quality." And they are not oblivious to their conditions.

> Examples of the negative memories reported were "I did not eat yesterday," "I had to have an operation," and "a relative died." In fact, of the seventy-three respondents who completed the memory measure, 20 mentioned poor health and 10 mentioned a friend or relative dying within the past year (347).

And yet, "the multiple measures approach to SWB research produced a picture of Calcutta's poor as a group that, while living in sub-standard conditions, are satisfied with many areas of their lives" (347). Drilling into these findings a bit, life satisfaction ratings were strongly correlated with income (344–345). The average life satisfaction ratings of the slum dwellers were in the positive range (2.23, where 2 is neutral) and only slightly lower than the scores reported by a control group of middle-class students at a Calcutta university (2.43) (341–345). Average life satisfaction ratings of the prostitutes (1.81) and homeless (1.60) were in the negative range (341). Participants were also asked to rate their satisfaction with respect to 12 different life domains (material resources, friendship, morality, intelligence, food, romantic relationship, family, physical appearance, self, income, housing, social life). The average scores for the slum dwellers and for the sex workers were in the positive range for all 12 items; the average scores for the homeless were in the positive range for 10 of the 12 items (all except material resources and housing).

The Calcutta study raises the problem of adaptive preferences, the natural tendency of people's attitudes and desires to acclimate to deprived, oppressive, or abusive circumstances. People who suffer searing injustice can come to accept, desire, and in some cases help perpetuate the very unjust practices from which they suffer—creating a self-perpetuating causal network of oppression. This raises fascinating and important theoretical and policy issues (Sen 1999, Nussbaum 2001, Khader 2011). But many of the psychological mechanisms responsible for adaptive preferences can be found in our everyday triumphs and tragedies.

Bereavement studies show that not everyone who loses a child or a spouse experiences intense grief. Wortman and Silver (1989) found that about 30% of parents showed no significant

depression after losing a child to Sudden Infant Death Syndrome. Lund et al. (1989) found that 82% of people gave positive SWB reports two years after losing a spouse. In a well-
known study, winning a large amount of money in a lottery led
to only slight increases in life satisfaction, 4.00 versus 3.81
among controls on a 5-point scale (Brickman, Coates, and
Janoff-Bulman 1978, 921). Research on prison life shows considerable adaptation after a period of adjustment. In a review
of 90 studies, Bukstel and Kilmann (1980) conclude that "the
findings do not unequivocally support the popular notion that
correctional confinement is harmful to most individuals"
(487). Among first-offenders "without marked antisocial ten-
dencies," a common pattern involves "an initial [negative] adjustment reaction to incarceration, followed by a period of successful adjustment with another mild psychological reaction
(e.g., 'short-timer's syndrome') occurring just prior to release."
What's more, "[i]nadequate, passive, and dependent individuals may respond favorably to confinement, as institutional life
is highly structured . . . with basic needs being met" (488).

Proponents of SWB instruments do not deny that SWB reports can be influenced by fleeting contextual factors. Nor do
they deny that they tend to adjust to the facts of our lives fairly
quickly. Rather, they argue that there is enough consistency in
the results delivered by SWB instruments for us to consider
them to be plausible measures of well-being or of important
components of well-being.

> Subjective well-being variables are thought to reflect the
> actual conditions in a person's life. Thus, when these condi-
> tions change, reports of SWB should change accordingly.
> Yet, because there is some degree of stability in these condi-
> tions, we should also expect SWB measures to be relatively
> stable over time (Diener, Scollon, and Lucas 2003, 203).

So on the one hand, there is some consistency in SWB reports across time because well-being is a reasonably stable condition (Diener and Larsen 1984, Magnus and Diener 1991, Sandvak, Diener, and Seidlitz 1993, Erhardt, Saris, and Veenhoven 2000). But on the other hand, SWB reports are sensitive, at least temporarily, to changes in life circumstances that plausibly influence well-being (Argyle 1999).

Let's turn to how the network theory would have us understand hedonic adaptation. The implication for SWB instruments will be a fairly moderate one. They have an important role to play in measuring happiness and well-being. But we should be careful about taking a narrow range of first-person life evaluations to be an accurate measure of a person's well-being. Psychologists have developed a wide array of well-behaved instruments— some relying on self-reports, some not—for measuring a broad spectrum of states that often appear in PCNs. When many such instruments converge on a coherent picture of a person's PCN or PCN fragment, we have good reason to be confident in the rough accuracy of this picture.

3. The Network Theory and Hedonic Adaptation

In trying to understand the hedonic adaptation results, it is useful to frame our discussion around two extreme theses to avoid.

a. Adaptation is a pure reporting phenomenon: People's SWB reports are stable even when their well-being changes drastically.

b. Adaptation is a pure well-being phenomenon: People's well-being is stable even when their objective situation changes drastically.

While the truth is somewhere in the middle, it is useful to articulate these simple views as foils, as well-defined views to avoid. Which view you are drawn to will largely depend on what you take well-being to be. Suppose Stan believes that well-being is a function of a person's subjective states—say he accepts the authentic happiness view. As long as people's life evaluations are informed and autonomous, Stan will take the hedonic adaptation results to show that the mind suffers the slings and arrows of outrageous fortune with surprising aplomb. Hedonic adaptation, for Stan, is mostly a well-being phenomenon. But Ollie believes that well-being is largely a function of objective states, at least some of which a person might not know much about—say he accepts an informed desire theory. If dramatic changes to objective states that determine a person's well-being do not produce dramatic changes in a SWB measure, Ollie would take that to be a problem with the SWB instrument. Hedonic adaptation, for Ollie, is largely a reporting phenomenon. To defend his view, Ollie might argue as follows: "Take a person who has suffered some catastrophe (a lost hand, paralysis, the death of a child). How much would she pay to undo that catastrophe? If the informed person would pay a lot, that implies that the catastrophe significantly undermined her well-being, no matter what any SWB instrument says."

On the question of how to interpret hedonic adaptation, the traditional approach to the study of well-being leads to stalemate. Those whose commonsense judgments incline them to subjective theories, like Stan, will tend to think that adaptation is more of a well-being phenomenon. Those whose commonsense judgments incline them to objective theories, like Ollie, will tend to think that adaptation is not primarily a well-being phenomenon but mostly a reporting phenomenon. The deadlock in philosophy metastasizes to psychology.

The inclusive approach breaks these stalemates of common sense. If we embrace the result of this approach, the network theory, we cannot derive an interpretation of hedonic adaptation, as Stan and Ollie try to do, by reasoning through the logical implications of our favored theory of well-being. Instead, the network theory takes the issue of how to interpret hedonic adaptation to be a scientific one: What role do hedonic adaptation and the mechanisms responsible for it play in promoting or inhibiting positive causal networks? Psychologists have proposed two promising families of interrelated mechanisms responsible for hedonic adaptation (Fredrick and Loewenstein 1999). Some work by reducing the intensity of our feelings in response to an emotional event. These are desensitization or affect-stabilizing mechanisms. Others work by recalibrating our standards of judgment. They raise or lower what we take to be the neutral or normal state when we evaluate our lives. Let's explore some of these mechanisms and then ask what implications they have for happiness and well-being.

3.1. Affect-Stabilizing Mechanisms

Psychologists argue that we possess a host of affect-stabilizing mechanisms that operate to render powerful emotional states, both positive and negative, short-lived. In some cases, we use conscious, deliberative regulation to stabilize our emotions. This is common with negative emotions. We take steps to improve our moods by exercising or watching an amusing movie. But we might sometimes regulate overly positive emotions on solemn occasions (a funeral, a church service) or when we want to concentrate on a task (Wilson, Gilbert, and Centerbar 2002, 214).[2]

---

2. For more affect-stabilizing mechanisms, see Robert Cummins (2010) and Cummins and Nistico (2002).

Wilson, Gilbert, and Centerbar propose a complex system of affect-stabilization mechanisms they call *ordinization* (2002, 215–219). Ordinization begins with our natural aversion to uncertainty. We are sense-making creatures. When faced with events of emotional power, we typically try to explain, give meaning to, or otherwise understand these events. Once an emotionally salient event is understood, it loses its affective charge. Suppose you experience an event of considerable emotional power—perhaps you are diagnosed with a serious illness or you get a big promotion. Your first emotional reaction is intense. After a short time, whenever you think about your new situation, and you think about it a lot, strong emotions wash over you. But after a while, you start to weave the event into the story of your life, understanding it, putting it into perspective, making sense of it. What's more, life intervenes. You start to focus on other tasks, large and small—taking the kids to soccer practice, finishing up a project at work, getting the kitchen painted—and these activities, to varying degrees, draw your attention away from the emotionally powerful event. You think about it less, and when you do, its emotional impact wanes. Over time, you come to consider the event as part of the background of your life, perhaps a very important part of the background, but not its central consuming fact. Ordinization mechanisms work to keep your emotions in a healthy range, not too euphoric and not too dysphoric (2002, 213).

3.2. The Recalibration of Life Satisfaction Judgments

Permanent or long-term changes to your life can raise or lower the standards you use to evaluate your life (Schwarz and Strack 1999). For example, soon after the shock of a big positive (negative) event, we might take this fact to be part of the target we are evaluating and so it might lead us to evaluate our lives more positively (negatively). But after some time, these factors come to form part of the background expectation against which we evaluate our lives. The standards we use to evaluate our lives recalibrate to this "new" normal. And so the presence of these factors no longer registers in our life evaluations. A suggestive piece of evidence concerns the effect of recall on SWB judgments. Recalling three positive recent events leads to higher SWB reports, and recalling three negative recent events leads to lower SWB reports. This is not surprising. But what happens if one recalls events that occurred long ago, at least five years earlier? The effect flips. Recalling positive events from long ago leads to lower SWB reports, and recalling negative events from long ago leads to higher SWB reports (Strack, Schwarz, and Gschneidinger 1985).

Recalibration works first and foremost on the evaluations we make of our lives. It is natural to think of recalibration as a lagging indicator of hedonic adaptation: After a shock, your emotions settle back to where they were before and recalibration follows—your life evaluations go back to where they were before. But this idea, that emotion is where the action is and judgment lags behind, is probably a mistake. Remember ordinization: the cognitive work of understanding and making sense of the emotionally salient event in your life comes first, and then the event begins to lose its emotional power. Hedonic adaptation is probably the result of a whole host of cognitive and affective mechanisms working hand-in-hand. We come to terms with an emotionally powerful event, our preferences start to align with our new situation, our judgments about our lives become more moderate, and this helps reduce the intensity of our feelings; and because we now feel less strongly about the event, our preferences align, our judgments subside. And so on. This sort of feedback loop is common in the psychological study of well-being.

3.3. Implications of Hedonic Adaptation

For any view that takes happiness to consist of positive mental states, adaptation raises the specter of the dreaded hedonic treadmill. If Calcutta slum dwellers are, on average, only a smidgen less happy than nearby middle-class college students, and if a bunch of demographic factors don't much influence our happiness, it would seem that there is little we can do to promote our happiness. So we find ourselves on a treadmill: Once free of atrocious circumstances, objective improvements in our lives cannot bring about long-term increases in happiness because adaptation snuffs them out. The pursuit of happiness becomes the absurd, exhausting exercise of trying to advance on a treadmill set to match our ever-increasing efforts.

But once we have a clear sense of what happiness and well-being are, the treadmill should not trouble us. Distinguish the intensity, the duration, and the frequency of happy episodes, episodes involving positive states of mind. The adaptation mechanisms we have reviewed place limits on the duration and intensity of happy episodes. But they do not seem to place any limits on their frequency. The only limits on the frequency of happy episodes are the usual ones imposed by our "too too solid flesh"—time, energy, and the vicissitudes of life. Hedonic adaptation is like an inefficient bouncer who throws you out of the party once you've had enough fun but who can't prevent you from picking yourself up, catching your breath, and coming right back in.

The situation with well-being is different. Our affect-stabilizing and recalibration mechanisms do not necessarily place significant constraints on the strength of our PCNs. In fact, from the perspective of the network theory, adaptation provides a reason for *optimism* about the prospects of robust, long-term well-being. Without these adaptation mechanisms, you might find yourself always in state of ecstasy and perpetually passing extremely positive evaluations on your life. While this might sound nice in theory, the prospect of becoming perpetually stuck in a state of unadulterated bliss is likely to hinder your long-term ability to operate effectively in the world. Our affect systems have a function. They serve to prepare us to deal with actual or potential environmental challenges and opportunities. Fear readies us for danger; disgust makes us avoid contaminants and disease; thirst and hunger orient us toward opportunities; and positive feelings and emotions reward us for success. Our affect systems are not perfectly designed for modern life, and so we fear spiders but not cars, and we seek out and enjoy foods that make us sick (Nesse and Williams 1996). An affect system that is always maximally engaged cannot effectively alert us to new challenges and opportunities or motivate us to act appropriately toward them.

An overheating emotional system would bring other disadvantages as well. It would expend considerable energy. And it would interfere with our ability to think clearly "as anyone knows who has tried to review a journal article while severely depressed or wildly in love" (Wilson, Gilbert, and Centerbar 2002, 213). For the hedonist, our inability to maintain intense pleasure over long periods of time might be dispiriting. And for the defender of the authentic happiness view, the tendency of our life evaluations to "reset" after positive life events might be disheartening. *But given the sort of creatures we are*, hedonic adaptation is crucial to our long-term successful functioning. It is essential to our ability to engage with the world in a way that promotes our positive causal networks. Hedonic adaptation is not a cause for pessimism or concern. It is essential to long-term well-being.

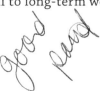

4. Objective Happiness

Daniel Kahneman has proposed an account of objective happiness, explicitly inspired by Bentham, that is based on the idea that a person's experience at a time has a certain utility, an objective value along a bipolar Good/Bad (GB) dimension. The GB dimension has a set of negative values, a neutral value, and a set of positive values. A person's objective happiness over a period of time is given by "the temporal integral of instant utility" (1999, 5). To take a simple example, suppose that over the course of 30 seconds, Joy experiences +3 units of objective happiness (OHs) per second for the first 10 seconds, +5 OHs per second for the next 10 seconds, and –4 OHs per second for the final 10 seconds. Over the course of the 30 seconds, Joy experienced 40 OHs (30 OHs + 50 OHs – 40 OHs). Kahneman suggests we measure where a person falls along the GB scale in terms of the extent to which she is engaged in activities she would rather continue than discontinue (1999, 4). So I am on the positive range of the GB scale if I prefer to continue what I am doing; and I am in the negative range of the GB scale if I prefer to discontinue what I am doing.

Philosophers have found fault with Kahneman's view of objective happiness. Anna Alexandrova, for example, argues that it is a mistake to suppose that a person's actual evaluations at a time are always accurate indicators of the person's genuine level of happiness at that time. In at least some cases, it is cool-headed, after-the-fact evaluations that best represent a person's overall happiness (2005, 307–311). Suppose Shad is in the grips of schadenfreude, feeling delight at another person's failure. Even though he might prefer to continue his schadenfreude experience, he might later disavow it as inappropriate and might, in fact, insist that it "was not really happiness" (308). Fred Feldman argues that it is a mistake to take a person's objective happiness to be a function of the strength of her desire to continue or discontinue her current experience. Suppose Helen wants to undergo a painful experience in order to serve penance or to receive a financial reward (2010, 42). Although Helen strongly desires to continue a deeply unpleasant experience, it is implausible to suppose she is objectively happy. These criticisms are successful on the assumption that Kahneman is offering a traditional philosophical theory of happiness, one that aims to capture our commonsense judgments about happiness. But I don't think Kahneman's notion of objective happiness is best understood along these lines.

Objective happiness is first and foremost an *explanatory* posit. It is supposed to explain how people's retrospective evaluations can misrepresent facts about the objective quality of their lives. Kahneman takes objective happiness (and unhappiness) to help explain two families of facts.

1. *Duration Neglect*: People tend to evaluate a painful experience (e.g., a colonoscopy or placing their hands in cold water) in terms of two moments, the peak pain experience and the end pain experience. The duration of the pain experience does not register in our evaluations (Redelmeier and Kahneman 1996). This seems to be a clear error of judgment: Other things being equal, one is better off experiencing pain A than experiencing pain A + B.
2. *Adaptation*: People's SWB evaluations are surprisingly insensitive to long-term changes to their objective circumstances. At least on occasion, this might seem to be an error of judgment: If both A and B are good things, other things being equal, one is better off with A + B than with just A.

If it is possible for a retrospective SWB evaluation to be wrong, there must be some facts that our SWB judgments are supposed to track. Kahneman posits objective happiness as the fact about which our SWB evaluations can be wrong.[3]

The explanatory purpose of objective happiness could be served by a brute "feel good" conception of happiness. This would fit nicely with the placeholder view defended earlier. But Kahneman rejects this proposal: "Philosophical discussions of the measurement of well-being . . . remind us of the common intuition that the evaluation of happiness is in part a moral judgment, which invokes a conception of the good life." He then offers a non-exhaustive list of the sorts of factors that make up objective happiness and that the GB scale should represent: the hedonic quality of current, remembered, and anticipated experience; current mood; flow; and involvement in current activities (1999, 6). These states, for Kahneman, are not identical to a person's well-being but rather are essential to it. "The concept of objective happiness is not intended to stand on its own and is proposed only as a *necessary element* of a theory of human well-being" (2000, 683, emphasis added).

My guess is that a simple brute "feel good / feel bad" conception of happiness and unhappiness would best serve Kahneman's explanatory purposes. But let's see if we can provide a coherent account of objective happiness so that (i) objective happiness includes Kahneman's non-exhaustive list of states (e.g., mood, flow, involvement in activities) and (ii) that objective

---

3. The network theory postulates PCNs as facts about which our SWB evaluations can be true or false. So if adaptation causes Angela's well-being judgments to remain stable even after her PCNs have become stronger, we have objective grounds on which to say that at least one of her well-being judgments is false. But the network theory cannot explain why Angela's claims about pain or ill-being are false. And so it cannot fully explain adaptation (since we adapt to negative events), and it cannot explain duration neglect (our tendency to ignore the duration of a painful event in evaluating it) at all. I do not press this partial solution here because it's not obvious that when a person makes a SWB report, that report is most charitably understood to be about well-being rather than something a person has better access to, such as happiness.

happiness is essential to well-being. The network theory can deliver the notion of objective happiness Kahneman seeks.

Objective Happiness: A person's objective happiness consists of states that (a) make up her PCN or PCN fragments and (b) have a positive hedonic tone.

I don't mean to suggest that this is what Kahneman had in mind when he proposed the notion of objective happiness. I don't even want to claim that he would endorse this interpretation of his view.[4] But this network theory-based interpretation of objective happiness has three virtues. It makes sense of some of the explanatory roles Kahneman takes objective happiness to play. It makes sense of much of what he explicitly says about objective happiness—for example, it is a necessary element of human well-being. And it allows Kahneman to evade some tough philosophical objections to his view.

The tough objections derive from Kahneman's proposal about how to measure the conglomeration of states that make up objective happiness. The difficulty of capturing everything that goes into the Good/Bad scale prompts Kahneman to operationalize objective happiness in terms of the extent to which one is engaged in activities one would rather continue than discontinue. Such a judgment is a reasonable, though not a perfect, measure of the strength of a person's objective happiness (or perhaps net objective happiness). If this is right, Kahneman does not take objective happiness to be made up of such judgments. Kahneman takes the fact that Shad wants his current schadenfreude to continue to be a sign, but not a sure sign, that it contributes to his objective happiness; he takes the fact that

4. To explain duration neglect, the fact that our evaluations of some painful events are insensitive to their duration, we would also need an account of objective unhappiness.

Helen wants the painful experience to continue to be a sign, but again not a sure sign, that it contributes to her objective happiness. Whether those states actually contribute to objective happiness will depend on whether they have a positive hedonic tone (which eliminates Helen's experiences) and whether they are part of a PCN or a PCN fragment (which may or may not eliminate Shad's schadenfreude).

A good theory should occasionally be able to improve upon promising and useful ideas. That has been my goal here: To show that from the perspective of the network theory, there is a fairly clear notion of objective happiness, it does important explanatory work, and it eludes some serious philosophical objections. The network theory cannot, of course, guarantee that objective happiness will be a central explanatory posit for Positive Psychology. That is for the scientists to settle. All a good theory of well-being can do—and this is not trivial—is make the best case for a promising idea like objective happiness.

5. Hedonic Set Points: Twin Studies and the Pursuit of Happiness

Hedonic adaptation can be at least partly explained in terms of affect-stabilizing mechanisms and the recalibration of life satisfaction judgments. Another oft-proposed explanation posits a genetically determined hedonic "set point"—a person's natural level of happiness. A person might be knocked off her set point in response to events, but this aberration is temporary. In absence of further shocks, one typically returns to one's natural set point (Headey and Wearing 1989, Stones and Kozma 1991). How powerful are genes in establishing this set point? Some have suggested that our genes entirely determine our set points. Lykken and Tellegen remark, "It may be that trying to be happier is as futile as trying to be taller and therefore is counterproductive" (1996, 189). Proponents of the set point hypothesis are typically more cautious. Indeed, Lykken reports that he regretted this remark "as soon as it appeared in print" (1997, 6). The typical claim is that a person's hedonic set point is genetically determined to a significant degree. Lyubomirsky, King, and Diener argue that 50% of a person's characteristic level of happiness over her life "is genetically determined and is assumed to be fixed, stable over time, and immune to influence or control" (2005, 116).

The appeal to genetic determination, even partial genetic determination, deserves careful scrutiny for two reasons. First, the claim is fairly common in the psychological literature (though not universal, see, e.g., Headey 2010) and in popular books written for non-specialists (e.g., Haidt 2006, Seligman 2007, Lyubomirsky 2008). And second, the claim that our long-term level of happiness is significantly "immune to influence or control" is deeply pessimistic. It suggests that interventions designed to improve our quality of life have limited potential. Psychologists try to soften the pessimistic impact in a number of ways. They argue that the set point is only partially genetically determined and so can be influenced by environmental factors; that genes fix a hedonic set point indirectly by shaping mechanisms that influence our dispositions to feel or to act; and that the set point for most people is in the "happy" range. Even with these qualifications, it is worth being clear about whether twin studies give us reasonable grounds for any pessimism at all about the prospects of bringing about long-term, stable improvements to our lives. I contend that they do not. There are serious and well-understood problems associated with extracting genetic determination conclusions from heritability evidence. What I will say about heritability is not new and it does not depend on the network theory. I focus on it here because given the current state of the evidence, it is important to resist the lure of genetic determination explanations for hedonic adaptation.

The first step to resisting this lure is to recognize that the claim that some trait is 50% genetically determined is deeply puzzling. Suppose Sonny's usual happiness level is 7 on a scale of 10. What does it mean to say that this set point is 50% genetically determined? Here are three false starts.

1. *Sonny's genes guarantee that he'll never veer below a 3.5.* It just can't be true that environmental circumstances are incapable of dragging Sonny's temporary levels of happiness below 50% of 7. Everyone occasionally suffers from the heartache and the thousand natural shocks that flesh is heir to.

2. *Sonny's genes give him a 50% chance of reaching a hedonic set point of 7.* This claim makes no sense in absence of assumptions about Sonny's environment. In an environment with an infant mortality rate of 60%, Sonny does not have a 50% chance of reaching a hedonic set point of 7.

3. *In a typical modern Western environment, Sonny has a 50% chance of reaching a hedonic set point of 7.* While this claim is more reasonable, it still can't be right. Putting aside the issue of what a "typical modern Western environment" is, we simply don't have the right sort of evidence to support this claim. We don't know whether 50% of people with Sonny's relevant suite of genes who find themselves in normal Western environments develop a hedonic set point of 7. And even if we did, this evidence by itself would not support any genetic determination conclusions. More than 50% of people in normal Western environments who have two X chromosomes wear their hair past their ears. But there is no plausible sense in which wearing long hair is more than 50% genetically determined.

These interpretations all go wrong in the same way. They assume that we can extract claims about a particular individual from heritability results. Heritability results by themselves cannot tell us anything about how Sonny's, or anyone's, genetic blueprint unfolds. To see this, let's turn to a twin study.

Take a trait that varies in a population, like height or income. The heritability of that trait in that population is a ratio, A/B. B is a measure of the trait's total variation in that population, and A is a measure of the trait's variation in that population that can be "accounted for" by genetics (where the scare quotes are meant to suggest that this cannot be understood at face value—more on this soon).

$$\frac{\text{Genetically produced diversity in population P}}{\text{Total diversity (genetically produced + environmentally produced diversity) in population P}}[5]$$

To say that the heritability of happiness in a population is 50% is to say that 50% of the variation in happiness in that population can be "accounted for" by genetics. Lykken and Tellegen (1996) gave self-report happiness surveys to 79 identical (monozygotic) twins and 48 fraternal (dizygotic) twins 10 years apart (at roughly age 20 and 30). Here are the crucial results.

Total diversity: The correlation between people's well-being scores at 20 and 30 (i.e., the within individual correlation over time) was .50. "The retest correlation for the WB scale was .50, indicating, as one would expect, that there is considerable fluctuation in one's sense of well-being, especially perhaps during the important transitional period from age 20 to 30" (188).

5. I should note that this is the "broad" heritability measure, h_b^2, rather than the "narrow" measure typically used by biologists. For an explanation of the difference, see Downes (2010).

Diversity among identical twins: The correlation between the well-being score of one identical twin at 20 and the other at 30 was .40.

Lykken and Tellegen conclude that "the heritability of the stable component of subjective well-being approaches 80%" (186). They figured the heritability of happiness by dividing the identical twin correlation (.40) by the overall correlation (.50). The intuitive idea here is that genes "account for" 80% of the total variation in happiness in this population. "Unshared environmental effects must then account for the remaining 20% of the variance in the stable component of happiness" (188).

This study suggests that the heritability of happiness is very high. But heritability is a notoriously tricky concept, and there are serious hurdles to drawing genetic determination conclusions from heritability evidence (e.g., Kitcher 1985, Block 1995, Downes 2010).

Genetic Determination: To say that trait T is "genetically determined" is to say that a person's genes will produce T in a very wide range of plausible environments. This is best understood in terms of norms of reaction (e.g., Lewontin 1974, Block 1995, Sober 1988). A norm of reaction describes how, for a particular genotype, T is expressed in varying environments. Rather than say that T is genetically determined, it is less misleading to say that T has a flat norm of reaction (Figure 6.1). And rather than say that T is not genetically determined (or is environmentally determined), it is less misleading to say that it has a sloped or curvy norm of reaction (Figure 6.2).

Heritability: To say that T is highly heritable is to say that most of the diversity in T in a particular population in a particular environment is genetic diversity, or rather, diversity that can be "accounted for" (scare quotes again) in terms of genetics.

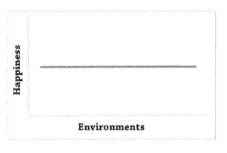

FIGURE 6.1

A Flat Norm of Reaction

Heritability tells us how much variation in happiness in *one particular population* in *one particular environment* is "accounted for" by genes. It doesn't tell us whether people's happiness levels are insensitive to a *wide range of environments*. Heritability is a measure that is relative to a-particular-population-in-a-particular-environment. This means that a trait might be highly heritable in one population but not in another. That's because heritability rises with increases in genetically produced diversity *and with*

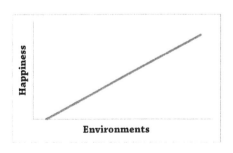

FIGURE 6.2

A Sloped Norm of Reaction

decreases in environmentally produced diversity. If Sonny lives in an environment that is homogeneous with respect to happiness-production (each person's environment is equally conducive to happiness), the heritability of happiness will be high. If Sonny lives in an environment that is heterogeneous with respect to happiness-production (there is a wide variation in how effectively different people's environments promote happiness), the heritability of happiness will be lower (Downes 2010, Haybron 2011b, fn. 19, Sosis 2014). *This is true even if Sonny leads exactly the same life in both environments.* It is inappropriate to draw causal conclusions about individuals (e.g., Sonny's happiness is to some degree genetically determined) from correlational evidence about populations that include those individuals (e.g., the heritability of happiness in some population is .50).

Against the speculation that the high heritability of happiness might be the result of environmental homogeneity, the defender of set points might reply with studies of twins raised apart. The happiness levels of identical twins raised apart are far more strongly correlated than the happiness levels of fraternal twins raised apart (Tellegen et al. 1988, 1035, Lykken and Tellegen 1996, 189). If genes do not play a significant role in fixing happiness, surely this difference would be negligible. Despite the intuitive pull of this argument, it is too quick. There is a puzzle about the set point hypothesis: Why is the heritability of happiness among fraternal twins so low? If our happiness levels are largely genetic, why are the happiness levels of fraternal twins about as correlated as the happiness levels of any two arbitrary people in this cohort? (Tellegen et al. report the correlations for fraternal twins raised apart is .18 and together is .23 [1988, 1035]; Lykken reports them as .13 ± .09 and .08 ± .04 [1997, 2].) Proponents of the set point hypothesis have offered a speculative hypothesis consistent with their view but, as far as I can tell, no firm evidence for it (Lykken et al. 1992). There is another speculative hypothesis that does not require set points and that explains the studies of twins raised apart. The homogeneity hypothesis is that the environments of identical twins are more homogeneous with respect to the promotion of happiness than the environments of fraternal twins. This is why the heritability of happiness for identical twins is higher than the heritability of happiness for fraternal twins.

Why would anyone think that the environment of identical twins raised apart is less diverse with respect to the promotion of happiness than the environments of fraternal twins raised apart? It is time to explain the scare quotes. So far, we have assumed that we can measure the variation in a trait in that population that can be "accounted for" by genetics. Suppose S's genes in her environment produce traits T1-Tn; what's more, S's genes would produce T1-Tn in a relatively wide range of environments besides her actual one. In other words, the norms of reaction for T1-Tn are flat. Suppose these traits include eye color, hair color, appearance, basic cognitive mechanisms (e.g., color vision), and some basic personality dispositions (e.g., extraversion). Consider two different processes by which S's genes might reliably influence S's typical levels of happiness in her environment.

Direct: (a) S's genes reliably produce T in a wide range of environments. T is an affect-stabilizing mechanism (or a suite of such mechanisms). T operates to place limits on the duration and intensity of hedonically charged episodes. (b) There is a reasonable degree of variation in the population in how affect-stabilizing mechanisms operate. The affect-stabilizing mechanisms of siblings or fraternal twins will show much greater variation than those of identical twins. (c) As a result of (a) and (b), the happiness of identical twins raised apart correlate more strongly than the happiness of fraternal twins raised apart.

Indirect: (i) S's genes reliably produce T in a wide range of environments. T is a *culturally valued trait*. It is a physical or psychological trait that is positively or negatively valued in S's culture. A different culture (or the same culture at a different time) might place a different value on T. Culturally valued traits might include physical attractiveness, certain physical traits (such as height, skin color, or hair color) or psychological traits (such as mathematical ability, verbal dexterity, extraversion, or shyness). (ii) There is a reasonable degree of phenotypic variation among culturally valued traits such that siblings typically have different culturally valued traits, (e.g., one sibling is male, the other is female; one sibling is taller, or darker skinned, or less verbally dexterous than another). (iii) Possessing traits that other people value and appreciate often promotes well-being. And so people who have genes that happen to produce traits that are more highly valued in their culture will tend to be happier, have greater well-being, and evaluate their lives more positively. (iv) Identical twins share more culturally valued traits than do fraternal twins. This explains why the happiness of identical twins raised apart correlates more strongly that the happiness of fraternal twins raised apart.

The homogeneity hypothesis is that a significant part of the reason happiness is heritable among identical twins but not among fraternal twins is that identical twins share more culturally valued traits than do fraternal twins (Block 1995, Sosis 2014).

Shyness is a possible example of a culturally valued trait. In a classic study (not involving twins), Caspi, Elder, and Bem (1988) analyzed longitudinal data on over 200 people born in 1928–1929. Shyness measures were taken when participants were children and again when they were about 30 years old. Men who were shy boys were more likely to delay marriage, children, and careers. "In all, men who were reluctant to enter social settings as children appear to have become adults who are more generally reluctant to enter the new and unfamiliar social settings" (827). Shy boys also had less professional success and stability as adults (827). "[H]aving [both] a history of shyness and entering a stable career late significantly raises the probability of being divorced or separated by midlife" (828). If identical twins are more alike in shyness than fraternal twins, this might partially explain why happiness correlates more strongly for identical twins raised apart than for fraternal twins raised apart.

There is an interesting twist to the shyness study. The above results did not generalize to women. Women who were shy children were not slower to marry or start a family compared to other women. At the time of marriage, the husbands of shy and non-shy women did not differ in occupational status. But the men who married shy women ended up having a higher occupational status than the men who married non-shy women.

> This suggests that shy women may actually have aided their husbands' careers by fulfilling the traditional homemaker role . . . Alternatively, of course, it may be that more ambitious or capable men marry shy or more domestically inclined women . . . The available data do not enable us to choose between these alternatives or among them and several other plausible scenarios (828–829).

It is a fascinating *cultural* fact that in mid-twentieth-century America, being naturally shy had different hedonic implications for men and women.

Is the homogeneity hypothesis true? There's surely something to it. I don't know whether it can explain the twin-study results fully or close to fully. But my thesis is not that the homogeneity hypothesis is true. My main goal has been to defend an agnostic optimism with respect to the genetic determination of happiness and well-being. Agnostic because we don't have enough evidence to reasonably draw any general conclusions about genetically determined set points. Optimism because we have evidence that there exist environments and interventions that promote well-being. An attitude of agnostic optimism is appropriate on both evidential and moral grounds. We know that some people's long-term happiness and well-being can be improved by changes to their behavior and environment. But how far does this optimism go? Is there an effective intervention for every person who needs one? Or are some people doomed by their genes to darkness and despair? The truth is, we don't know. But we do know that we have only just begun exploring interventions—environmental, behavioral, therapeutic, and medical—that might effectively promote people's happiness and well-being. Until we have exhausted all the options, until we have good reason to give up hope, we should proceed on the assumption that there is hope for all.

6. Conclusion

The arguments in this book run along two tracks. The first track argues for lots of views about well-being and happiness. The second aims to display the advantages of an approach to the study of well-being that stand even if I'm wrong about the first-track arguments. The inclusive approach integrates philosophy and psychology in a way that makes the investigation into the nature of well-being look like a fairly routine instance of scientific practice. It adopts a respectful attitude toward the theoretical speculations of philosophers, the empirical investigations of psychologists, and everyone's commonsense judgments. Of course, this deferential attitude can only go so far. Where there are genuine disagreements, some people are going to be wrong. In this chapter, I have tried to argue that the network theory can help to clarify and sometimes broker substantive disputes in Positive Psychology. It naturally delivers a view of happiness that fits smoothly with current happiness research (the placeholder view); it provides a natural way to understand Kahneman's notion of objective happiness; it strikes a plausible balance between optimism and pessimism about the status of SWB instruments; and it backs two explanations for adaptation (affect-stabilizing mechanisms and the recalibration of satisfaction judgments).

I have ignored some issues in Positive Psychology that one might reasonably expect a useful theory to help clarify. Two deserve special mention. I have ignored what psychologists have said about the nature of well-being. This is to avoid repetition, as psychologists tend to defend versions of theories I criticized in chapter 5—hedonism, authentic happiness, or Aristotelian theories (Tiberius 2006). The second issue I have overlooked, with regret, is the role of Positive Psychology in public policy. Traditionally, governments have measured people's quality of life using various objective economic and social indicators (such as GDP, literacy rates, longevity, rates of poverty). But there has been a growing movement to employ measures that are allegedly more sensitive to people's happiness and well-being. This important topic is too large to do it justice here. But this chapter can be understood as an attempt to defeat some initial reasons for pessimism about the prospects of using public policy as a tool to improve people's happiness and well-being. The case for pessimism can be built on three premises:

1. We possess powerful affect-stabilizing mechanisms that limit our happiness once we are above the poverty line.
2. Our evaluative standards recalibrate quickly to the facts of our lives, which prevents us from maintaining extremely positive evaluations of our lives.
3. Each of us has a happiness "set point" that is significantly determined by our genes.

The pessimist will grant that social and institutional policies that lift people out of terrible conditions can significantly reduce ill-being. And the importance of reducing ill-being is not to be underestimated. But the pessimist contends that our adaptive capacities imply that social and institutional policies that change the objective conditions of people's lives cannot bring about stable, long-lasting improvements to people's well-being.

The network theory does not endorse these grounds for pessimism. Hedonic adaptation does not restrict the frequency of a person's happy episodes. In fact, hedonic adaptation is likely to be essential to our long-term well-being. What's more, there is strong evidence that public policy can bring about long-term improvements in the quality of people's lives (Trout 2009, Conley 2013). The network theory provides a framework for understanding the mechanisms by which policy influences the dynamics of well-being. Policies that promote physical and psychological health can establish PCN prerequisites (states that are necessary for any PCN). Policies that open up opportunities for success—academic, professional, economic, interpersonal, and so forth—can establish PCN essentials (states that are necessary for certain types of

PCN) as well as causal drivers of PCNs (states that tend to establish, maintain, or strengthen PCNs). Policies can establish and strengthen PCNs and thereby promote long-term well-being. The network theory provides a clear and intuitive account of the relationship between successful public policy and well-being. Figuring out how it fits with well-established views in this area is a job for another day.

Chapter 7

Objections to the Network Theory

In this book, I have defended three views.

1. A view about how to study well-being: an inclusive approach that asks a theory of well-being to answer to both common sense and science.
2. A view about the science of well-being: Positive Psychology is the study of the structure and dynamics of positive causal networks (PCNs).
3. A view about the nature of well-being: Well-being consists of PCNs and PCN fragments. A person's degree of well-being is a direct function of the strength of her PCN and PCN fragments.

I have not paused much over doubts and objections. This is for two reasons. First, the inclusive approach guarantees that the case for any theory will be cumbersome. We must assess the theory and its leading competitors in terms of how well they explain a diverse range of evidence. The argumentative line was tricky enough without getting waylaid by objections. The second reason I have so far ignored objections is that my replies are often of the "yes, but" variety. They rely on the *relative merits* of the network theory compared to its competitors. Of course, this reply is available only after the case for the relative merits of the network theory is in place.

This chapter considers three objections to the network theory. The first is that it has counterintuitive implications. I have already tipped my hand with respect to this family of objections. Some philosophers wedded to the traditional approach might find the "yes, but" reply maddening. But given the diversity of philosophers' commonsense judgments, no successful theory can capture every expert's intuitions. So the theory that deserves our support is the one that best captures the totality of the evidence. And that, I contend, is the network theory. The second objection is supposed to apply to all plausible theories of well-being. Thomas Scanlon has argued that well-being is an inclusive good, useless for first-person deliberation (1998a, 1998b). I will argue that the network theory explains both the power and the flaw in Scanlon's argument. The third objection is likely to trouble many philosophers: Well-being is supposed to be good or valuable. How can the network theory account for the *normativity* of well-being, the fact that S's well-being is *valuable* for S? Philosophers understand normativity in different ways. I will argue that the network theory is able to explain the value of well-being on some plausible ways of understanding normativity.

1. Counterintuitive Cases

Philosophers are trained to develop counterexamples to theories. And they're good at it. So the philosopher's first move against the network theory will be to present cases in which it delivers a counterintuitive judgment about well-being. Although I'm sure to miss some powerful counterexamples, I propose to grant up front that the network theory will have some implications you find counterintuitive. Heck, it has implications *I* find counterintuitive. My response to such cases will be familiar by now: Many of us have some very firmly held commonsense judgments about well-being that are wrong. To pass the bar that has been set by common sense, a theory merely has to capture our pretheoretical judgments reasonably well. Whether a theory deserves our allegiance depends on how well it explains the entirety of the evidence, both the evidence of common sense and of science. And by that standard, the network theory excels. Let's start with a counterexample that aims to show that having a robust PCN is not necessary for well-being.

> *The Lucky*: Hap instantiates a very robust PCN, so according to the network theory Hap has a high degree of well-being. Luc has exactly the same positive experiences, attitudes, traits, and accomplishments as Hap. Yet for Luc, these experiences, attitudes, traits, and accomplishments are not causally connected in a way that makes them a network. There are a number of ways this might happen. Perhaps Luc is on an incredible run of good fortune. Or perhaps Luc's positive affect is not caused by his successes but by H-radiation that just happens to hit the right parts of his brain, and while he has virtues and works hard, his accomplishments are not the result of his virtues or hard work. Luc is just lucky. Or perhaps Luc's life is guided by a deity who intervenes at random times to bring him good things.

The defender of the network theory might reject this class of counterexamples as farfetched. But this move is doomed. It depends on the critic not being able to come up with more realistic counterexamples. And philosophers are very resourceful counterexample generators. But even if the only counterexamples to

the network theory are unrealistic, the philosopher is unlikely to
see this as particularly damning. Few philosophers think hedonism is off the hook because the experience machine is unrealistic. So the network theory must address this objection as long as
someone like Luc is possible—as long as it's possible for someone
to have a life that looks just like Hap's, both from his perspective
and the perspective of an onlooker who is blind to the underlying causal structure of their lives, but without the PCN.

In response to this class of counterexamples, the defender of
the network theory should appeal to PCN fragments. While Luc
does not have the PCN that Hap does, he does possess PCN fragments that are made up of the same states as Hap's PCN. And
since the network theory takes well-being to be a function of
PCN fragments, it can deliver the intuitive judgment in this case
(assuming it is your intuitive judgment): Luc has a high degree of
well-being because of the strength of his PCN fragments. Every
counterexample I can think of that calls into question whether
PCNs are necessary for well-being can be overcome in this same
way. As long as Luc's PCN fragments, all told, are made up of the
same states as Hap's PCN, the network theory will imply that
Luc has a high degree of well-being.

Let's turn to cases in which having a PCN seems to be not
sufficient for well-being: One can have a PCN and not have
well-being. I'm sure others will be able to come up with more intuitively powerful cases than the ones I present. But I will stick
to fairly simple cases because, in the end, there is no getting
around the fact that the network theory will violate some people's commonsense judgments.

The Thriving Wicked: We have already considered the case
of Josef, a wicked sadistic man with a robust PCN (chapter 2). He instantiates a causal network involving feelings, attitudes, traits, and interventions in the world

that are "successful" in the sense that they consist of positive experiences for Josef and are valued by Josef and his culture. This seems to be a real possibility, particularly in sick societies (think Mengele).

According to hedonism, the network theory, and the informed desire theory Josef has a high degree of well-being. But the Aristotelian, as well as the defender of any plausible moralized view of well-being, will take the opposite view. From the perspective of the network theory, *Wicked* is an extreme example of an important truth. The contours of well-being—more concretely, the states that tend to be causal drivers of PCNs—depend critically on cultural conditions. The typical profile of a person high in well-being is likely to differ across cultures. For example, people high in well-being in individualist cultures tend to have greater self-esteem than people high in well-being in collectivist cultures (Diener and Suh 2000). The network theory explains this diversity. Cultural norms and practices can play a causal role in what sorts of states tend to promote PCNs. Recall that PCNs were defined, in part, in terms of states that are valued by the person's culture. The more a culture values self-esteem, the more likely self-esteem is to be praised, endorsed, and rewarded; and so the more likely it is to promote PCNs. *Wicked* takes this point to its natural extreme. In a culture in which cruelty is rewarded, a person naturally disposed to cruelty can have success and a high degree of well-being. This is not a consequence to jump for joy about. It's just a sobering fact about our world that bad people can have well-being.

Let's consider two more counterexamples that take PCNs to not be sufficient for well-being.

Numb Ned: Ned is very good at faking happiness. As a result, he gets all the social benefits of being upbeat and happy. People like him, are more generous toward him, and so forth. While Ned instantiates a robust PCN, he is numb inside. He experiences neither positive nor negative feelings.

Sad Sam. Sam is very good at faking happiness. As a result, he gets all the social benefits of being upbeat and happy. People like him, are more generous toward him, and so forth. While Sam instantiates a robust PCN, he is very sad. He experiences no positive feelings, only negative ones.

It would seem that the network theory takes Ned and Sam to have a high degree of well-being. And many will find these implications contrary to common sense. Various maneuvers might muffle the intuitive shock the network theory produces in these cases. I propose to test out some of these maneuvers in the hope that they might placate some people's commonsense judgments. But I am under no illusions. These maneuvers don't even placate all of my commonsense judgments.

For the network theory, what makes a causal network a positive one is that it consists of relatively more states that feel good or are valued (either by the person or the culture). If Sam and Ned never feel good, then perhaps these networks are not positive at all. And so the network theory will not have any counterintuitive consequences for those who take Sam and Ned to not have well-being. This line of defense won't hold for long. That's because the proponent of these counterexamples can stipulate that while the PCNs do not have any links that feel good, they do have many links that are valued by the respective individuals and their cultures. And so the theory would be committed to Sam and Ned both having well-being. At this point, the proponent of the network theory can try to turn the tables. If Sam and Ned's PCNs consist of many links that they and their cultures endorse, value, and respect, is it really so obvious that they do not have well-being? If Sam and Ned appreciate and value their many friends, their loving families, their successful careers, and what they do every day, and these states are connected in a cascading cycle of accomplishment, it is perhaps not implausible to suppose with the network theory that anyone with such a rich, full life must have well-being.

Fred Feldman has proposed an example somewhat reminiscent of *Numb* that is relevant here.

> Stoicus just wants peace and quiet. He wants to live an unruffled life. We must be clear about Stoicus's desires: it's not that he wants peace and quiet because he thinks these will give him sensory pleasure. He wants peace and quiet as ends in themselves. In fact, he prefers not to have sensory pleasure. He prefers not to have sensory pleasure in part because he fears that if he had some sensory pleasure, it would ruffle his life. He feels the same way about sensory pain: he does not want it.
>
> Suppose Stoicus gets exactly what he wants—peace, quiet, no sensory pleasure, and no sensory pain. Suppose that as he receives his daily dose of peace and quiet, Stoicus is pleased. That is, suppose he enjoys the peace and quiet. Suppose he takes attitudinal pleasure in various facts about his life, including the fact that he is not experiencing any sensory pleasure. Suppose Stoicus eventually dies a happy man. He lived 90 years of somewhat boring but on the whole quite enjoyable peace and quiet. Stoicus thinks (right before he dies) that his has been an outstandingly good life (Feldman 2002, 610).

Feldman takes Stoicus to be an example of someone with well-being but without any pleasant states. Does the network theory side with Feldman on the Stoicus case? We can't tell because the case is too underdescribed to know whether Stoicus has a PCN. (This is not a criticism of Feldman, as he meant this case to be a counterexample to sensory hedonism, not the network theory.) To be a counterexample to the network theory, we need to know what Stoicus does with his time. How does his life hang together? There must be some explanation of his ability to live in peace and quiet consistently over decades. Most of the ways I can imagine this occurring (e.g., Stoicus is a monk or a successful artist) would likely involve PCNs or PCN fragments. But unless these sorts of details are filled in, it is impossible to know how the network theory would judge the case.

Some people's commonsense judgments will rebel at the prospect of Stoicus or Ned having well-being. The case of sad Sam is likely to face even stronger opposition. But the defender of the network theory has one more maneuver to assuage, at least somewhat, these violations of common sense. As a matter of psychological fact, people are limited in their ability to convincingly feign happiness over a long period of time and in a wide range of situations. So even if *Numb* and *Sad* described psychologically possible cases, the PCNs of Ned and Sam would not be robust. And so for the network theory they would have a rather modest degree of well-being. This judgment will not satisfy those who take Sam and Ned to not have well-being, but it might somewhat dampen the shock to their pretheoretical intuitions. In reply to this attempt to limit the damage, the opponent of the network theory can stipulate that Sam and Ned have extraordinary, perhaps even superhuman, abilities to fake happiness over decades and in a wide range of circumstances. In that case, given the robustness of their PCNs, the theory is forced to judge them to have a high degree of well-being. But given this stipulation, the proponent of the network theory can once again try to turn the tables. Think about Sam and Ned. They are able to fake happiness so well that they deceive their closest friends, their spouses, their parents, and their children for decades. How can they do this? They must be so psychologically foreign that it becomes difficult to judge whether or not they have well-being. I am undecided, or perhaps just confused, about whether superhuman Sam and superhuman Ned have well-being. Of course, my judgment might be idiosyncratic or tainted by my bias. So let me just admit that the commonsense judgments of many readers are crystal clear and implacably opposed to the network theory: Sam and Ned do not have one iota of well-being.

In cases where common sense is deadlocked, confused, or even violated, it is important to have a clear sense of what we want from a theory of well-being. It is here that the inclusive approach carries a heavy load. It takes common sense to be only one line of evidence a theory of well-being must capture. Like its competitors, the network theory contradicts many people's commonsense intuitions, including my own, usually in very contrived, bizarre cases. The inclusive approach suggests we not judge these theories too harshly for these failures. Ultimately, the network theory deserves our allegiance because it is far better than its competitors at explaining the entirety of the evidence.

2. Well-Being as an Inclusive Good

Thomas Scanlon defends a hybrid view of well-being, according to which a person's well-being is a function of (i) her succeeding in her rational, comprehensive goals, (ii) her positive experiences, and (iii) her success in worthwhile or excellent activity (1998a). A useful way to think about Scanlon's view is that it co-opts the intuitive power of hedonism by taking well-being to be a function of pleasure, Aristotle's theory by taking well-being to be a function of excellent activity, and something like an informed desire theory by taking well-being to be a function of satisfying rational comprehensive goals. Scanlon argues that the move to such goals is an improvement on informed desire theories: "the idea that success in one's rational aims contributes to one's well-being can account for a number of the intuitions that have seemed to support informed desire theories while avoiding most of these theories' implausible implications" (1998a, 107). It seems doubtful that Scanlon's theory can organize and unify Positive Psychology as well as the network theory, given that it is essentially comprised of theories that fail to organize and unify Positive Psychology as well as the network theory. But I will not press that point here. Rather, I want to focus on Scanlon's contention that well-being is not a useful concept for first-person deliberation.

Central to Scanlon's argument is the idea that well-being is an inclusive good—"one that is made up of other things that are good in their own right, not made good by their contributions to it" (1998a, 120). As a result, "the idea of one's own well-being is transparent. When we focus on it, it largely disappears, leaving only the values that make it up" (1998a, 129). This transparency is what makes well-being unimportant in first-person deliberation.

> If you ask me why I listen to music, I may reply that I do so because I enjoy it. If you asked why that is a reason, the reply, "A life that includes enjoyment is a better life," would not be false, but it would be rather strange. Similarly, it would be odd to explain why I strive to succeed in philosophy by saying that my life will be a better life if I am successful in my main aims, insofar as they are rational. Again, this is true, but does not provide the right kind of reason. It would make more sense to say that I work hard at

philosophy because I believe it is worthwhile, or because I
enjoy it, or even because I long for the thrill of success. But
it would be empty to add that these things in turn are desir-
able because they make my life better (1998a, 119–120)

Scanlon's idea is that there are many perfectly reasonable factors to consider in deciding upon a course of action. But well-
being is not one of them because any appeal to well-being can be
eliminated in favor of far more informative and specific factors
(e.g., enjoyment, the thrill of success). In first-person decision-
making, the appeal to well-being is otiose, since I can and should
make decisions based on more concrete values and considerations. Well-being is an unenlightening stand-in for the specific
reasons that motivate me to act.

The crucial point about Scanlon's argument is that it applies
to our commonsense notion of well-being. So Scanlon's argument, if sound, motivates the inclusive approach. Put aside the
diversity of common sense. Even if there is a single commonsense concept of well-being shared by every person, Scanlon's
argument suggests that it suffers from a serious defect: It cannot
profitably inform our first-person practical deliberations. I suggest that the right reply to Scanlon is to abandon the traditional
approach, or any approach that inevitably commits us to this
flawed concept of well-being. The inclusive approach has the potential to deliver a theory that revises our commonsense understanding of well-being, and that revised concept might play a
helpful role in first-person practical deliberation. The inclusive
approach cannot guarantee this result. But if something like the
network theory is close to the mark, we have reason to be optimistic that an accurate concept of well-being will not suffer from
the ills Scanlon identifies in the commonsense concept.

The network theory allows us to diagnose both why Scanlon's
argument is so powerful and why it doesn't work. Start with the

premise that effective practical deliberation focuses on the dynamics of PCNs. Suppose I'm trying to decide whether to begin meditating. On the one hand, learning to meditate will take practice. And this will cut into time I could spend with my family or friends. What's more, I might find parts of the learning experience frustrating, so frustrating, in fact, that I quit before getting any benefits from the activity. On the other hand, there is evidence that meditation can promote states that I think would establish or strengthen my PCN: reduction of stress and depression, greater trust and acceptance of others, and fewer interpersonal problems (Shapiro, Schwartz, and Santerre 2002). My deliberations about the dynamics of PCNs might go wrong in various ways. Perhaps the studies showing that meditation has these benefits are faulty; or perhaps meditation has these benefits for many people but not for me; or perhaps the near-term effects of meditation on my life—lower stress, greater trust—would actually backfire and lead to my undoing. But these are standard, everyday failures of deliberation. They do not raise any special philosophical problems for the network theory as a theory of well-being.

The real problem is that the network theory's description of first-person deliberation seems to confirm Scanlon's view. My deliberations never explicitly advert to my well-being. I wonder whether meditation will improve my mental life; whether this will strengthen my relationships or boost my performance at work; whether these accomplishments will tend to further promote a positive, healthy mental life; and whether, via these sorts of feedback loops, meditation will help bring about a stable, long-term improvement to the quality of my life. Effective practical deliberation needs only to focus on the causal powers of the states that make up our PCN or potential PCNs. Pondering these dynamical questions is crucial to practical deliberation. And if competently done, thinking through such dynamical questions can lead to more effective deliberations and more successful action. And so from the perspective of the network theory, Scanlon's contention that well-being disappears from effective first-person practical deliberation is compelling. But I don't think it's true. That's because for the network theory, to deliberate about the structure and dynamics of PCNs *is* to deliberate about the structure and dynamics of well-being. Alternatively, to say one is deliberating about PCNs but not well-being is like saying one is theorizing about the element with 10 protons in its nucleus but not neon. If you're talking about PCNs (or the element with atomic number 10), you're talking about well-being (or neon) whether you know it or not. And so well-being, properly understood, is not irrelevant to effective practical deliberation. It is central to such deliberation.

The network theory holds that a person's level of well-being is determined by the strength of her PCN and PCN fragments. This is offered as an account of the nature of well-being. It is also offered as an improvement on our commonsense understanding of well-being. This sort of empirically informed conceptual revision is familiar in science. Science updates many of our concepts (e.g., whale, salt, forces, atoms, gravity) so that they fit smoothly into a successful empirical framework. A natural side effect of the inclusive approach is that our concept of well-being is likely to be reshaped so as to fit smoothly with the empirical study of the good life. In this way, it is reasonable to hope that it will come to be ever more useful in our explanations, in our predictions, and in our attempts to intervene effectively in the world.

3. The Normativity of Well-Being

Philosophers standardly describe a person's well-being as something intrinsically valuable for that person. To say that a person has a high degree of well-being is to say something normative. And so to pass muster, many philosophers will insist that the network theory satisfy the normativity requirement.

The normativity requirement: The network theory must explain why S's well-being is valuable for S.

The key problem with this requirement is that philosophers disagree about what normativity comes to. Many philosophers understand value in a rich sense, while others understand it in a slimmer, more modest sense. Whether the network theory can explain normativity will depend to a large extent on what we take normativity to be.

3.1. Normativity for the Network Theory: A First Pass

The network theory explains well-being in purely descriptive terms. It posits the existence of causal networks—homeostatically clustered emotions, attitudes, dispositions, and activities. Some of these networks are made up of states that are valued, that have a positive hedonic tone, or that tend to bring about states that are valued or have a positive hedonic tone. The network theory's appeal to what a person or culture "values" is entirely descriptive. There is a fact of the matter about what a person *actually* values. This can be measured in terms of what she is disposed to endorse, praise, pursue, or explicitly say she values.

If we begin with the rather simple idea that what is valuable is what is valued, then the network theory accounts for normativity. But since what people actually value can be distorted, sick, or otherwise mistaken, most philosophers will reject this view of normativity as not appropriately *normative*. One might amend the network theory, replacing the descriptive "what people actually value" with "what is actually valuable."[1] But this would make the network theory a moralized theory of well-being. And I have argued that moralized theories do not account for the empirical evidence as well as the network theory.

A more promising idea for the network theory begins with a well-known form of normative realism. According to Richard Boyd, what it is to be good or valuable in a genuinely normative sense is nothing more than to instantiate certain homeostatically clustered states.

> There are a number of important human goods, things which satisfy important human needs. . . . Under a wide variety of (actual and possible) circumstances these human goods (or rather instances of the satisfaction of them) are homeostatically clustered. . . . Moral goodness is defined by this cluster of goods and the homeostatic mechanisms which unify them. Actions, policies, character traits, etc. are morally good to the extent to which they tend to foster the realization of these goods or to develop and sustain the homeostatic mechanisms upon which their unity depends (Boyd 1988, 203).

On this view, by describing the positive causal networks that "well-being" refers to and that satisfy many of our important needs, the network theory thereby also accounts for the normativity of well-being. Besides more fully clarifying the nature of PCNs, there is nothing else the network theory needs to do, or in fact can do, to account for normativity.[2]

---

1. I think the resulting theory would look something like the substantive theory of well-being Stephen Darwall defends in chapter 4 of *Welfare and Rational Care* (2002).

2. Footnote 2 of Richard's Boyd classic paper, "How to be a Moral Realist," sketches an outline of something much like the network theory of well-being (1988, 204).

The network theory satisfies the normativity requirement given Boyd's rather slim conception of it. But many philosophers will insist on something more robust. My goal here will be to consider some alternative conceptions of normativity that might be plugged into the normativity requirement. For each alternative, I will argue that either the network theory can satisfy the demand or its failing to satisfy the demand is not a good reason to reject the theory.

3.2. Non-Naturalism and the Meaning Demand

G. E. Moore famously proposed the open-question argument for thinking that goodness, and value in general, is non-natural. For any account of goodness framed in terms of purely natural, descriptive properties, D, it can always be meaningfully asked whether D is good (Moore, 1903/1993). "Is D good?" is an open question in the sense that it is not settled by our understanding its component terms. With respect to the network theory, the relevant open question is: "Is Betty's positive causal network intrinsically good for Betty?" Given our ordinary, commonsense understanding of "well-being," this is an open question. But what are we supposed to conclude from that fact? As many philosophers have noted, if the conclusion of the open question argument is that an identity statement is false, the argument is fallacious. Water is H_2O even though, before we discovered the real nature of water, it was an open question whether water is H_2O. And so the state of well-being might be identical to the state of instantiating a PCN even if we cannot know this by a detailed examination of our ordinary understanding of "well-being."

Other philosophers, particularly proponents of non-cognitivism (the view that normative claims are not capable of being true or false) sometimes use the open-question argument to come to a semantic conclusion. For example, Allan Gibbard employs the argument to suggest that a descriptive, Humean account of rationality "is wrong as a claim about meaning" (1990, 12). And so here is one way to understand the normativity requirement.

> *The meaning demand*: The network theory must account for the meaning of "well-being" in a way that captures the fact (made clear by the open-question argument) that the meaning of "well-being" is not exhausted by any purely descriptive content.

This is not a legitimate demand. A theory about the nature of well-being is no more required to account for the ordinary meaning of "well-being" than a theory about the nature of water is required to account for the ordinary meaning of "water." The meaning demand is inappropriate because it reverses the proper relationship between the meaning of a term and the nature of what the term denotes. Ultimately, it is the correct theory about the nature of well-being that should drive how we understand well-being.

Grant for the sake of argument that the semantic version of the open-question argument is sound and everyone understands well-being in a non-cognitivist way. This is consistent with the network theory because it is not a theory about the meaning of "well-being." It is a theory about what well-being is. And given the truism that we should understand well-being (or anything, really) in terms of what it actually is, a theory about the nature of well-being might recommend that we revise our everyday understanding of it. The network theory implies that well-being claims can be true or false. Of course, the non-cognitivist might argue for a different theory about the nature of well-being, a theory that does not have this result. But the case for an alternative theory cannot be won entirely on the basis of the commonsense evidence. Given the inclusive approach, the only way to show that another theory is better than the network theory is to slog through the scientific evidence and prove it.

3.3. The Objective Reason Demand

One way to interpret the normativity challenge assumes that genuinely normative claims have some sort of authority over us, even if we explicitly reject that authority. If doing A will promote my well-being, then I have an objective or categorical reason to do A, a reason that stands even if I lack any desire or motivation to do A (Scanlon 1998b, Parfit 2011). This objective reason is usually understood to be a *prima facie* reason, which means that it might be outweighed by other reasons. The stop sign gives me a prima facie reason to stop, but I have a stronger reason not to stop since I'm driving an ambulance, siren blaring, to go save someone's life and no other vehicles or pedestrians are around.

> *The objective reason demand*: The network theory must explain why S has objective prima facie reasons to promote her well-being.

The notion of objective reasons is difficult and obscure. It's not clear such reasons exist, and if they do, it's not clear what they involve. Any account of objective reasons is bound to be controversial. The notion of objective reasons is obscure enough that I don't know whether the network theory can satisfy the demand. So plug any account of objective reasons into the above demand. Either the network theory satisfies the demand or it does not. If it satisfies the demand, it stays. And if it does not, then we must choose between the network theory and the demand. As long as there is strong evidence for the network theory and it is considerably less controversial than the demand, then it is the demand that must go. To elaborate a bit, suppose we are considering two ideas:

- a theory of well-being that has strong evidential support, and
- an account of objective reasons that makes it the case that S doesn't have objective prima facie reasons to promote her well-being.

In this situation, it is a mistake to give up on the more solid theory of well-being. Either we reject the account of objective reasons or we conclude, perhaps counterintuitively, that we don't always have objective prima facie reasons to promote our well-being. (This is an example of a "yes, but" reply to an objection. It assumes that the evidence of science and common sense supports the network theory. If the case for the theory collapses, then whether or not it can satisfy the objective reason demand hardly matters.)

3.4. The Motivation Demands

The normativity requirement is sometimes framed in terms of the question, "Why should I care?" This is familiar in discussions of Plato's Ring of Gyges and Hume's sensible knave. The Ring of Gyges, introduced in Plato's *Republic*, is a ring that makes its wearer invisible, and so capable of engaging in immoral behavior without fear of getting caught. Hume's sensible knave is a clearheaded amoralist who claims to be unmoved by appeals to conscience, sympathy, fellow-feeling, honor, justice, or morality. In both cases, the issue is how to convince someone to behave morally: If the person can get away with an action that benefits him without detection, why should he care that it's immoral? If we take the normativity requirement to involve answering the amoralist's challenge, then we are assuming that what makes well-being valuable is that it is intrinsically motivating. If doing A will promote my well-being and I fully understand this, I will have some motivation to do A. I might have countervailing motivations to do something else, of course, in which case I might not actually do A. But my well-being must be, to at least some degree, intrinsically motivating.

> *The unrestricted motivation demand*: S understands what well-being is and what would promote S's well-being. The network theory must explain why S has (or must have) some motivation to promote his well-being.

The reason this demand seems so hard to satisfy is that some people appear to be completely unmotivated to pursue their well-being. And in fact, this is what makes the demand an unreasonable one. The only theory that can satisfy the unrestricted motivation demand is a theory that identifies well-being only with states people are actually motivated to pursue. The existence of self-hating, self-destructive people implies that any theory that satisfies this demand is bound to yield some well-being judgments that are, from the perspective of common sense, grotesque. So no intuitively plausible theory *ought* to be able to satisfy the unrestricted demand. Even if we put this problem aside, however, there are further considerations for thinking that the unrestricted motivation demand is unreasonable.

If I insist on copping an attitude of sullen obstreperousness, no theory can make me care about anything—morality; justice; rationality; artistic achievement; or my good health, reputation, or well-being. It is absurd to reject a theory because it is possible for someone with a bad attitude to not care what the theory says. No one would think to reject a theory about the nature of atoms because Sullen Sid cares not a whit about atoms. We do not reject evolution because no power on Earth can make Grumpy Gus care about evolution. And there is no good reason to reject a theory about the nature of well-being (or justice or morality) because we can't talk a sensible knave into caring about it. This doesn't mean that the philosophical project of trying to identify the amoralist's mistake, if there is one, is worthless. If I had a new and plausible proposal, I would have told it to you by now. My point is that it is unreasonable to require that a theory of anything be able to convince people to care about it who are dead-set on not caring about it.[3]

To make the motivation demand more plausible, we might restrict it to rational people.

> *The rational motivation demand*: S is a rational person who understands what well-being is and what would promote S's well-being. The network theory must explain why S will be at least somewhat motivated to promote her well-being.

There are a number of ways to understand rationality here. A Humean would take rationality to involve the efficient satisfaction of one's goals. This means–end rationality might also require that a person's goals be based on beliefs and deliberations that are in some way idealized (e.g., coherent, fully informed). Whatever the details, insofar as a person's self-hatred or self-destructiveness can survive informed and coherent beliefs, the Humean demand will suffer the same fate as the unrestricted demand. It is an inappropriate demand because no intuitively plausible theory ought to satisfy it. That's not to say that the Humean, means–end view of rationality is false. It is only to say that some

---

3. I should note that many philosophers would frame the motivation demand in terms of reasons. I will not do this in order to avoid confusion with the objective reason demand. But I do not mean to take a stand on the internalism–externalism debate about reasons.

means–end rational agents are not motivated to promote their well-being. And so no true theory can explain why they are.

The rational motivation demand might employ a non-Humean account of rationality (Korsgaard 1996). But such views are quite controversial. Just as with the objective reason demand, failing to satisfy a demand this controversial cannot sink a theory that has a lot of evidence in its favor. Plug any account of rationality into the rational motivation demand. If the network theory cannot satisfy it, it is the more controversial demand that we should reject. We should keep the more solid theory of well-being and give up either the account of rationality or the assumption that every rational person is motivated to pursue her well-being.

There is a way to modify the motivation demand so that the network theory can satisfy it. Restrict the demand to normal agents (Dreier 1990).

> *The normal person motivation demand*: S is a normal person who understands what well-being is and what would promote S's well-being. The network theory must explain why S will be at least somewhat motivated to promote her well-being.

The network theory satisfies this demand on any intuitively plausible interpretation of what counts as a "normal" person. It is characteristic of a normal person to be at least somewhat motivated to pursue activities that establish, strengthen, or maintain positive causal networks, that is, networks consisting of states she tends to find pleasurable and valuable. It would be strange for someone to be completely cold to the prospect of a life of accomplishment, personal or professional or both, which promotes good feelings, attitudes, and dispositions, which in turn promotes further accomplishments, and so on.

3.5. The Normativity Requirement, Revisited

The network theory takes well-being to be a homeostatic property cluster of states that is the referent of our expression "well-being," that satisfies important human needs, and that normal people are motivated to pursue. On more than one conception of normativity—Boyd's normative realism and a motivation demand restricted to normal people—these facts are the basic elements that explain why well-being is valuable. Other than spelling out these facts in more detail, not a trivial task, the network theory has nothing else to do to satisfy the normativity requirement.

The nature of value is a deeply controversial topic, and many philosophers will be dissatisfied with the form of normativity the network theory delivers. But then it is reasonable to ask: What alternative form of normativity is it supposed to deliver? We have considered five other possibilities. Three—the meaning demand, the unrestricted motivation demand, and the Humean rational motivation demand—are inappropriate. No plausible theory about the nature of well-being should be expected to satisfy them. And the other two—the objective reason demand and the non-Humean rational motivation demand—are controversial. In fact, they are too controversial to overturn any theory of well-being that is well supported by the evidence.

Now, the dissatisfied philosopher might argue that there are many sophisticated views of normativity in the literature, and some of these might trip up the network theory. True enough. But my main goal here has been to articulate the network theory's basic strategy for handling the normativity requirement: Argue that it can explain why well-being is valuable given some plausible ways to understand normativity. Given any other clear account of normativity that can be plugged into the normativity requirement, the network theory can handle it in one of three ways.

1. It meets the requirement.
2. It fails to meet the requirement but the requirement is illegitimate because no plausible theory should be expected to meet it.
3. It fails to meet the requirement but the requirement is controversial enough that the network theory's failing to meet it does not undermine the theory.

Until there is a plausible form of the normativity requirement that the network theory cannot meet *and* that is on firmer evidential grounds than the network theory, it is reasonable to conclude that the network theory satisfies the normativity requirement.

Chapter 8

Conclusion

The study of well-being suffers because philosophy and psychology are estranged. Without facts, philosophers find themselves lost and at loggerheads amid the swamps of common sense. And without a good theory of well-being, psychologists find that they cannot clearly and plausibly explain what Positive Psychology is about. One lesson of this book is that what philosophers and psychologists can't do on their own, they can do together. To be successful, the study of well-being must be a genuinely joint venture. Discovering its nature requires the knowledge and skills of both the philosopher in her armchair and the scientist in her lab. On the inclusive approach, we figure out what well-being is by identifying the item in the world that makes sense of the science of well-being and that makes most of our common-sense judgments about well-being true. This approach is radical insofar as it shakes up how philosophers have traditionally studied well-being and conventional insofar as it is based on assumptions that have been standard in philosophy of science for decades.

The inclusive approach frees the philosopher from the mires of common sense and yields a new theory of well-being, the network theory. Well-being consists of positive causal networks

(PCNs) and their fragments. PCNs are networks of emotions, attitudes, traits, and behaviors that tend to be self-maintaining and self-reinforcing. They include experiences that feel good and states that the individual or her culture values. The strength of a person's well-being is a direct function of the strength of her PCN and PCN fragments. The network theory explains well-being in purely descriptive terms. The state of well-being is metaphysically on a par with the state of being depressed or suffering from heat stroke. These conditions have a causal and dynamical structure that scientists can measure, study, and interfere with.

The inclusive approach also provides the psychologist with a much-needed framework for understanding the science of well-being. It is the study of the structure and dynamics of positive causal networks. Psychologists who investigate well-being are constantly uncovering PCN fragments—relationships among positive emotions, attitudes, traits, and successful interactions with the world. And they sometimes step back and describe the ways in which these states tend to feed back on themselves to create "upward spirals." In other words, they are studying well-being and its component parts. The description I have offered of PCNs is inelegant but serves its purpose—to identify what the scientific study of well-being is about.

This book is the first step in a larger project, a project that naturally branches off in both practical and theoretical directions. Any plausible moral or political theory needs an account of human well-being, given that individuals and governments at least sometimes have a duty to promote it. I think that the views defended here fit most comfortably within a naturalistic framework for understanding human value, one that interprets our moral practices to be first and foremost a natural product of social, psychological, and biological forces (e.g., Kitcher 2011). But this is not compulsory. The network theory can profitably supplement a wide range of moral and political theories.

Well-being is interesting for theoretical reasons, but the main reason Positive Psychology has attracted so much attention in recent years is because it seems to promise scientifically sound advice about how to promote well-being. The unclarity that resides at the heart of Positive Psychology—the confusion as to what it is about—inevitably infects its recommendations. A psychologist tells you that engaging in a new activity will make your life better. Better how? If the advice is designed merely to bump up your life evaluations a bit, it might be terrible advice. Life evaluations do not always track how well our lives are going. Few of us would trade places with a Calcutta slum dweller, even if after a period of adjustment this were to slightly boost our life evaluations. Another psychologist tells an employer that a new corporate practice will improve her company's health and well-being. But what does this mean? That it will improve the company's bottom line? This might be a reason for the employer to adopt the practice, but why should those of us not sharing in the company's profits think this is wise advice? Further, what is distinctive about the psychologist's advice? How is it different from the advice a corporate analyst might give? A third psychologist tells us that implementing a new government program will promote the general welfare. But again, what concrete value is being promoted? If the new program improves people's mood without bringing any durable improvements to their lives, dumping a few tons of mood-enhancing drugs into the nation's water supply might do the trick. If Positive Psychology is merely pushing such superficial "Doctor Feelgood" benefits, we shouldn't take it or its advice seriously.

The network theory gives us a way past these objections. Positive Psychology is not the psychology of superficial pleasure, blind optimism, life evaluations, rugged individualism, or the latest self-help fad. It is the study of positive causal networks. Discoveries about the dynamics of positive causal networks— what factors tend to establish, inhibit, maintain, or strengthen such networks—naturally lead to practical recommendations. If you want to establish or strengthen positive causal networks, do *this*. If you don't want to weaken or destroy positive causal networks, don't do *that*. Of course, not every recommendation psychologists propose will work. Applying new knowledge to the world is hard. But when it's right, Positive Psychology offers advice that helps groups or individuals establish, maintain, or strengthen positive causal networks.

If we understand well-being along the lines suggested by the network theory, well-being is objectively valuable. It is a legitimate factor to consider when an individual, organization, or government is deciding what to do. That doesn't mean it's always the weightiest consideration. John might rightly sacrifice his well-being to care for his ailing mother, and an organization or government might properly implement a policy that protects the rights of a minority regardless of whether it promotes the general welfare.

Some will worry that the network theory, by taking well-being to be something real and objective, will inevitably foist on us a narrow, parochial view of the good life. The exact opposite is true. The science of well-being shows that both interpersonal and intrapersonal positive causal networks can take root in a diverse range of cultures and ways of life. If we happen to live in a society in which only a privileged few can achieve well-being, that's a problem with our society, not the science of well-being. In fact, it is a problem that the science of well-being can help solve by reminding us of the many ways well-being can be realized, by giving us advice about how to give more people more opportunities to achieve well-being, and by testing and refining that advice. Finally, a well-founded science of well-being can explain the value it seeks to achieve: people becoming "stuck" in cascading cycles of feelings, attitudes, habits, traits, and accomplishments that build on each other and that they find pleasant and valuable. That sounds like a good life, doesn't it?

REFERENCES

Abbe, Allison, Chris Tkach, and Sonja Lyubomirsky. 2003. "The Art of Living by Dispositionally Happy People." *Journal of Happiness Studies* 4: 385–404.

Alexandrova, Anna. 2005. "Subjective Well-Being and Kahneman's 'Objective Happiness'." *Journal of Happiness Studies* 6: 301–324.

———. 2012. "Well-Being as an Object of Science." *Philosophy of Science* 79: 678–689.

Angner, Erik. 2010. "Subjective Well-Being." *Journal of Socio-Economics* 39: 361–368.

Argyle, Michael. 1999. "Causes and Correlates of Happiness." In D. Kahneman, E. Diener, and N. Schwarz, eds., *Well-Being: The Foundations of Hedonic Psychology*, 353–373. New York: Russell Sage Foundation.

Aristotle. 2000. *Nichomachean Ethics*. Translated by Roger Crisp. Cambridge: Cambridge University Press.

Babyak, Michael, James A. Blumenthal, Steve Herman, Parina Khatri, Murali Doraiswamy, Kathleen Moore, W. Edward Craighead, Teri T. Baldewics, and K. Ranga Krishnan. 2000. "Exercise Treatment for Major Depression: Maintenance of Therapeutic Benefit at 10 Months." *Psychosomatic Medicine* 62: 633–638.

Baron, Robert A. 1977. *Human Aggression*. New York: Plenum.

———. 1984. "Reducing Organizational Conflict: An Incompatible Response Approach." *Journal of Applied Psychology* 69: 272–279.

———. 1987. "Mood Interviewer and the Evaluation of Job Candidates." *Journal of Applied Social Psychology* 17: 911–926.

Baron, Robert A., Suzanne P. Fortin, Richard L. Frei, Laurie A. Hauver, and Melisa L. Shack. 1990. "Reducing Organizational Conflict: The Role of Socially-Induced Positive Affect." *The International Journal of Conflict Management* 1: 133–152.

Barsade, Sigal G., Andrew J. Ward, Jean D. F. Turner, and Jeffrey A. Sonnenfeld. 2000. "To Your Heart's Content: A Model of Affective Diversity in Top Management Teams." *Administrative Science Quarterly* 45: 802–836.

Bartholomew, Kim, and Leonard Horowitz. 1991. "Attachment Styles Among Young Adults: A Test of a Four-Category Model." *Journal of Personality and Social Psychology* 61: 226–244.

Berlyne, Daniel E. 1954. "A Theory of Human Curiosity." *British Journal of Psychology* 45: 180–191.

Benard, Bonnie. 1991. *Fostering Resiliency in Kids: Protective Factors in the Family, School, and Community*. Portland, OR: Western Center for Drug-Free Schools and Communities.

Berridge, Kent C., and Morton L. Kringelbach. 2013. "Neuroscience of Affect: Brain Mechanisms of Pleasure and Displeasure." *Current Opinion in Neurobiology* 23: 294–303.

Berry, Diane S., and Jane Sherman Hansen. 1996. "Positive Affect, Negative Affect, and Social Interaction." *Journal of Personality and Social Psychology* 71: 796–809.

Bishop, Michael. A., and J. D. Trout. 2013. "Prognosis and Prediction." In Bill Fulford, ed., *Handbook of the Philosophy of Psychiatry*, 1023–1046. New York: Oxford University Press.

Biswas-Diener, R., and Ed Diener. 2001. "Making the Best of a Bad Situation: Satisfaction in the Slums of Calcutta." *Social Indicators Research* 55: 329–352.

Block, Ned. 1995. "How Heritability Misleads about Race." *Cognition* 56: 99–128.

———. 2005. "Two Neural Correlates of Consciousness." *Trends in Cognitive Sciences* 9: 46–52.

Borgonovi, F. 2008. "Doing Well by Doing Good: The Relationship Between Formal Volunteering and Self-Reported Health and Happiness." *Social Science & Medicine* 66: 2321–2334.

Boyd, Richard N. 1988. "How to be a Moral Realist." In G. Sayre-McCord, ed., *Essays on Moral Realism*, 181–228. Ithaca, NY: Cornell University Press.

———. 1989. "What Realism Implies and What It Does Not." *Dialectica* 43: 5–29.

Bradburn, Norman M. 1969. *The Structure of Psychological Well-Being*. Chicago: Aldine Publishing Company.

Brandt, Richard B. 1979. *A Theory of the Good and the Right*. Oxford: Clarendon Press.

Brennan, Kelly A., and Jennifer K. Bosson. 1998. "Attachment-style Differences in Attitudes Toward and Reactions to Feedback from Romantic Partners: An Exploration of the Relational Bases of Self-Esteem." *Personality and Social Psychology Bulletin* 24: 699–714.

Brennan, Kelly A., and Phil R. Shaver. 1995. "Dimensions of Adult Attachment, Affect Regulation and Romantic Relationship Functioning." *Personality and Social Psychology Bulletin* 21: 267–284.

Brickman, Philip, Dan Coates, and Ronnie Janoff-Bulman. 1978. "Lottery Winners and Accident Victims: Is Happiness Relative?" *Journal of Personality and Social Psychology* 36: 917–927.

Bukstel, Lee H., and Peter R. Kilmann 1980. "Psychological Effects of Imprisonment on Confined Individuals." *Psychological Bulletin* 88: 469–493.

Burger, Jerry M., and David F. Caldwell. 2000. "Personality, Social Activities, Job-Search Behavior and Interview Success: Distinguishing Between PANAS Trait Positive Affect and NEO Extraversion." *Motivation and Emotion* 24, 1: 51–61.

Burns, David D. 1980. *Feeling Good: The New Mood Therapy*. New York: Wm. Morrow and Co.

Cameron, R. J. 2003. "Applied Positive Psychology: Enhancing Resilience in Vulnerable Children and Young People." In J. Henry, ed., *European Positive Psychology Proceedings*. Milton Keynes: Open University.

Cameron, Kim S., David Bright, and Arran Caza. 2004. "Exploring the Relationships Between Organizational Virtuousness and Performance." *American Behavioral Scientist* 47: 766–790.

Campbell, Angus, Philip E. Converse, and Willard L. Rodgers. 1976. *The Quality of American Life: Perceptions, Evaluations, and Satisfactions*. New York: Russell Sage Foundation.

Cantril, Hadley. 1965. *The Pattern of Human Concerns*. New Brunswick, NJ: Rutgers University Press.

Carnelley, K. B., P. R. Pietromonaco, and K. Jaffe. 1994. "Depression, Working Models of Others, and Relationship Functioning." *Journal of Personality and Social Psychology* 66: 127–140.

Carver, Charles S., Michael F. Scheier, and Jagdish K. Weintraub. 1989. "Assessing Coping Strategies: A Theoretically Based Approach." *Personality and Social Psychology* 2: 267–283.

Caspi, Avshalom. 2003. "Influence of Life Stress on Depression: Moderation by a Polymorphism in the 5-HTT Gene." *Science* 301, 5631: 386–389.

Caspi, Avshalom., Glen H. Elder Jr., and Daryl J. Bem. 1988. "Moving Away From the World: Life-Course Patterns of Shy Children." *Developmental Psychology* 24: 824–831.

Clark, Daniel M. 1986. "A Cognitive Model of Panic." *Behavior Research and Therapy* 24: 461–470.

Conly, Sarah. 2013. *Against Autonomy: Justifying Coercive Paternalism.* Cambridge: Cambridge University Press.

Costa, Paul, and Robert R. McCrae. 1980. "Influence of Extraversion and Neuroticism on Subjective Well-Being: Happy and Unhappy People." *Journal of Personality and Social Psychology* 38: 668–678.

Côté, Stéphane. 1999. "Affect and Performance in Organizational Settings." *Current Directions in Psychological Science* 8: 65–68.

Crisp, Roger. 2006. "Hedonism Reconsidered." *Philosophy and Phenomenological Research* 73: 619–645.

Crowell, Judith, R. Chris Fraley, and Philip R. Shaver. 1999. "Measures of Individual Differences in Adolescent and Adult Attachment." In J. Cassidy and P.R. Shaver, eds., *Handbook of Attachment: Theory, Research and Clinical Applications,* 434–465. New York: Guilford Press.

Csikszentmihalyi, Mihaly. 2008. *Flow: The Psychology of Optimal Experience.* New York: Harper Perennial.

Cummins, Robert A. 2000. "Personal Income and Subjective Well-Being: A Review." *Journal of Happiness Studies* 1: 133–158.

———. 2010. "Subjective Wellbeing, Homeostatically Protected Mood and Depression: A Synthesis." *Journal of Happiness Studies* 11: 1–17.

Cummins, Robert A., and Helen Nistico. 2002. "Maintaining Life Satisfaction: The Role of Positive Cognitive Bias." *Journal of Happiness Studies* 3: 37–69.

Cunningham, Michael. 1988. "Does Happiness Mean Friendliness? Induced Mood and Heterosexual Self-Disclosure." *Personality and Social Psychology Bulletin* 14: 283–297.

Danner, Deborah D., David A. Snowdon, and Wallace V. Friesen. 2001. "Positive Emotions in Early Life and Longevity: Findings from the Nun Study." *Journal of Personality and Social Psychology* 80: 804–813.

Darwall, Stephen. 2002. *Welfare and Rational Care.* Princeton: Princeton University Press.

De Brigard, Felipe. 2010. "If You Like it, Does It Matter if It's Real?" *Philosophical Psychology* 23: 43–57.

De Moor, M. H. M., A. L. Beem, J. H. Stubbe, D. I. Boomsma, and E. J. C. De Geus. 2006. "Regular Exercise, Anxiety, Depression and Personality: A Population-Based Study." *Preventive Medicine* 42: 273–279.

DeNeve, Kristina M., and Harris Cooper. 1998. "The Happy Personality: A Meta-Analysis of 137 Personality Traits and Subjective Well-Being." *Psychological Bulletin* 124: 197–229.

Diener, Ed. 1984. "Subjective Well-Being." *Psychological Bulletin* 95, 3: 542–575.

Diener, Ed, and Carol Diener. 1996. "Most People are Happy." *Psychological Science* 7, 3: 181–185.

Diener, Ed, Robert A. Emmons, Randy J. Larsen, and Sharon Griffin. 1985. "The Satisfaction with Life Scale." *Journal of Personality Assessment* 49: 71–75.

Diener, Ed, and Randy J. Larsen. 1984. "Temporal Stability and Cross-Situational Consistency of Affective, Behavioral, and Cognitive Responses." *Journal of Personality and Social Psychology* 47: 871–883.

Diener, Ed, C. Nickerson, R. E. Lucas, and E. Sandvik. 2002. "Dispositional Affect and Job Outcomes." *Social Indicators Research* 59: 229–259.

Diener, Ed, C. Scollon, and R. Lucas. 2003. "The Evolving Concept of Subjective Well-Being: The Multifaceted Nature of Happiness." *Advances in Cell Aging and Gerontology* 15: 187–219.

Diener, Ed, and Martin E. P. Seligman. 2002. "Very Happy People." *Psychological Science* 13: 81–84.

Diener, Ed, and Eunkok M. Suh. 2000. *Culture and Subjective Well-Being*. Cambridge, MA: MIT Press.

Doris, John M. 2002. *Lack of Character: Personality and Moral Behavior*. Cambridge: Cambridge University Press.

Downes, Stephen M. 2010. "Heritability." In E. N. Zalta, ed., *The Stanford Encyclopedia of Philosophy* (Fall 2010 Edition). http://plato. stanford.edu/archives/fall2010/entries/heredity/.

Dreier, Jamie. 1990. "Internalism and Speaker Relativism." *Ethics* 101: 6–26.

Duckworth, Angela L., Christopher Peterson, Michael D. Matthews, and Dennis R. Kelly. 2007. "Grit: Perseverance and Passion for Long-Term Goals." *Journal of Personality and Social Psychology* 92: 1087–1101.

Dutton, Jane, Mary Ann Glynn, and Gretchen Spreitzer. 2006. "Positive Organizational Scholarship." In J. Greenhaus and G. Callahan, eds., *Encyclopedia of Career Development*, 641–644. Thousand Oaks, CA: Sage.

Dutton, Donald G., Keith Saunders, Andrew Starzomski, and Kim Bartholomew. 1994. "Intimacy-Anger and Insecure Attachment as Precursors of Abuse in Intimate Relationships." *Journal of Applied Social Psychology* 24: 1367–1386.

Easterlin, Richard A. 1973. "Does Money Buy Happiness?" *The Public Interest* 20: 3–10.

———. 1995. "Will Raising the Income of All Increase the Happiness of All?" *Journal of Economic Behavior and Organization* 27: 35–47.

Erhardt, J. J., W. E. Saris, and R. Veenhoven. 2000. "Stability of Life Satisfaction Over Time: Analysis of Change in Ranks in a National Population." *Journal of Happiness Studies* 1: 177–205.

Feldman, Fred. 2002. "The Good Life: A Defense of Attitudinal Hedonism." *Philosophy and Phenomenological Research* 65: 3.

———. 2010. *What Is This Thing Called Happiness?* Oxford: Oxford University Press.

Ferguson D. P., G. Rhodes, K. Lee, and N. Sriram. 2001. "'They All Look Alike to Me': Prejudice and Cross-Race Face Recognition" *British Journal of Psychology* 92: 567–577.

Finnis, John. 1980. *Natural Law and Natural Rights*. New York: Oxford University Press.

Foot, Philippa. 2002. *Virtues and Vices: And Other Essays in Moral Philosophy*. New York: Oxford University Press.

Fredrick, Shane, and George Loewenstein. 1999. "Hedonic Adaptation." In D. Kahneman, E. Diener, and N. Schwarz, eds., *Well Being: The Foundations of Hedonic Psychology*, 302–329. New York: Russell Sage.

Fredrickson, Barbara. 1998. "What Good are Positive Emotions?" *Review of General Psychology* 2: 300–319.

———. 2001. "The Role of Positive Emotions in Positive Psychology: The Broaden-and-Build Theory of Positive Emotions." *American Psychologist* 56, 3: 218–226.

Fredrickson, Barbara, and Christine Branigan. 2005. "Positive Emotions Broaden the Scope of Attention and Thought-Action Repertoires." *Cognition and Emotion* 19: 313–332.

Fredrickson, Barbara, and Thomas Joiner. 2002. "Positive Emotions Trigger Upward Spirals Toward Emotional Well-Being." *Psychological Science* 13: 172–175.

Friedman, H.S. 1993. "Personality and Longevity: Paradoxes." In J. Robine, B. Forette, C. Franceschi, and M. Allard, eds., *The Paradoxes of Longevity*, 115–122. Berlin: Springer.

Frisch, M., Michelle P. Clark, Steven V. Rouse, M. David Rudd, Jennifer K. Paweleck, Andrew Greenstone, and David A. Kopplin. 2005. "Predictive and Treatment Validity of Life Satisfaction and the Quality of Life Inventory." *Assessment* 12: 66–78.

Gable, Shelly L., and Jonathan Haidt. 2005. "What (and Why) is Positive Psychology?" *Review of General Psychology* 9S: 103–110.

Gaines, Stanley O., Jr., Harry T. Reis, Shandra Summers, Caryl E. Rusbult, Chante L. Cox, Michael O. Wexler, William D. Marelich, and Gregory J. Kurland. 1997. "Impact of Attachment Style on Reactions to Accommodative Dilemmas in Close Relationships." *Personal Relationships* 4: 93–113.

Gibbard, Allan. 1990. *Wise Choices, Apt Feelings*. Oxford: Clarendon Press.

Griffin, James. 1986. *Well-Being: Its Meaning, Measurement, and Moral Importance*. Clarendon: Oxford.

———. 2007. "What Do Happiness Studies Study?" *Journal of Happiness Studies* 8: 139–148.

Griffiths, Paul E. 1997. *What Emotions Really Are*. Chicago: University of Chicago Press.

Gurin, Gerald, Joseph Veroff, and Sheila Field. 1960. *American View Their Mental Health: A Nation-Wide Interview Study*. New York: Basic Books.

Haidt, Jonathan. 2006. *The Happiness Hypothesis: Finding Modern Truth in Ancient Wisdom*. New York: Basic Books.

Harker, Lee Anne, and Dacher Keltner. 2001. "Expressions of Positive Emotion in Women's College Yearbook Pictures and Their Relationship to Personality and Life Outcomes Across Adulthood." *Journal of Personality and Social Psychology* 80, 1: 112–124.

Hassmen, Peter, Nathalie Koivula, and Antti Uutela. 2000. "Physical Exercise and Psychological Well-Being: A Population Study in Finland." *Preventive Medicine* 30: 17–25.

Haybron, Daniel M. 2003. "What Do We Want from a Theory of Happiness?" *Metaphilosophy* 34: 305–329.

———. 2007. "Life Satisfaction, Ethical Reflection, and the Science of Happiness." *Journal of Happiness Studies* 8: 99–138.

———. 2008. *The Pursuit of Unhappiness: The Elusive Psychology of Well-Being*. New York: Oxford University Press.

Haybron, Daniel M. 2011a. "Taking the Satisfaction (and the Life) Out of Life Satisfaction." *Philosophical Explorations* 14, 3: 249–262.

———. 2011b. "Happiness." In E. N. Zalta, ed., *The Stanford Encyclopedia of Philosophy* (Fall 2011 Edition). http://plato.stanford.edu/archives/fall2011/entries/happiness/.

Hazan, Cindy, and Philip Shaver. 1987. "Romantic Love Conceptualized as an Attachment Process." *Journal of Personality and Social Psychology* 52, 3: 511–524.

Headey, Bruce. 2010. "The Set Point Theory of Well-Being Has Serious Flaws: On the Eve of a Scientific Revolution?" *Social Indicators Research* 97: 7–21.

Headey, Bruce, Ruut Veenhoven, and Alex Wearing. 1991. "Top-Down Versus Bottom-Up Theories of Subjective Well-Being." *Social Indicators Research* 24: 81–100.

Headey, Bruce, and Alexander Wearing. 1989. "Personality, Life Events, and Subjective Well-Being: Toward a Dynamic Equilibrium Model." *Journal of Personality and Social Psychology* 57, 4: 731–739.

Heath, R. G. 1972. "Pleasure and Brain Activity in Man. Deep and Surface Electroencephalograms During Orgasm." *Journal of Nervous and Mental Disease* 154: 3–18.

Hurka, Thomas. 1993. *Perfectionism*. New York: Oxford University Press.

Hursthouse, Rosalind. 2002. *On Virtue Ethics*. New York: Oxford University Press.

———. 2013. "Virtue Ethics." In E. N. Zalta, ed., *The Stanford Encyclopedia of Philosophy* (Fall 2013 Edition). http://plato.stanford.edu/archives/fall2013/entries/ethics-virtue/.

Isen, Alice M. 1970. "Success, Failure, Attention, and Reaction to Others: The Warm Glow of Success." *Journal of Personality and Social Psychology* 15, 4: 294–301.

Isen, Alice M., Kimberly A. Daubman and Gary P. Nowicki. 1987. Positive Affect Facilitates Creative Problem Solving. *Journal of Personality and Social Psychology* 52, 6: 1122–1131.

Isen, Alice M., and Paula F. Levin. 1972. "Effect of Feeling Good on Helping: Cookies and Kindness." *Journal of Personality and Social Psychology* 21, 3: 384–388.

Johnson, Kareem J., and Barbara L. Fredrickson. 2005. "'We All Look the Same to Me': Positive Emotions Eliminate the Own-Race Bias in Face Recognition." *Psychological Science* 16, 11: 875–881.

Jones, R. Stewart. 1979. "Curiosity and Knowledge." *Psychological Reports* 45: 639–642.

Judge, Timothy A., and Chad A. Higgins. 1998. "Affective Disposition and the Letter of Reference." *Organizational Behavior and Human Decision Processes* 75, 3: 207–221.

Kagan, Shelly. 1998. *Normative Ethics*. Boulder, CO: Westview Press.

Kahneman, Daniel. 1999. "Objective Happiness." In D. Kahneman, E. Diener, and N. Schwarz, eds., *Well-Being: Foundations of Hedonic Psychology*, 3–25. New York: Russell Sage Foundation Press.

———. 2000. "Experienced Utility and Objective Happiness: A Moment-Based Approach. In D. Kahneman and A. Tversky, eds., *Choices, Values and Frames*, 673–692. New York: Cambridge University Press and the Russell Sage Foundation.

Kahneman, Daniel, and Angus Deaton. 2010. "High Income Improves Evaluation of Life but Not Emotional Well-Being." *Psychological and Cognitive Sciences* 107, 38: 16489–16493.

Kant, Immanuel. 1964. *The Doctrine of Virtue: Part II of the Metaphysics of Morals*. Translated by M. J. Gregor. Philadelphia: University of Pennsylvania Press.

Kashdan, Todd B., Robert Biswas-Diener, and Laura A. King. 2008. "Reconsidering Happiness: the Costs of Distinguishing between Hedonics and Eudaimonia." *The Journal of Positive Psychology* 3, 4: 219–233.

Kavka, Gregory. 1986. *Hobbesean Moral and Political Theory*. Princeton, NJ: Princeton University Press.

Keelan, J. Patrick R., Karen K. Dion, and Kenneth L. Dion. 1994. "Attachment Styles and Heterosexual Relationships Among Young Adults." *Journal of Social and Personal Relationships* 11, 2: 201–214.

Kesebir, Pelin, and Ed Diener. 2008. "In Pursuit of Happiness: Empirical Answers to Philosophical Questions." *Perspectives on Psychological Science* 3, 2: 117–125.

Keyes, Corey L. M., and Jonathan Haidt. 2003. *Flourishing: Positive Psychology and the Life Well-Lived*. Washington, DC: American Psychological Association.

Khader, Serene J. 2011. *Adaptive Preferences and Women's Empowerment*. New York: Oxford University Press.

Kitcher, Philip. 1985. *Vaulting Ambition: Sociobiology and the Quest for Human Nature*. Cambridge, MA: MIT Press.

———. 1990. "The Division of Cognitive Labor." *Journal of Philosophy* 87, 1: 5–22.

———. 2011. *The Ethical Project*. Cambridge, MA: Harvard University Press.

Knobe, Joshua, and Shaun Nichols, eds. 2008. *Experimental Philosophy*. New York: Oxford University Press.

———, eds. 2013. *Experimental Philosophy: Volume 2*. New York: Oxford University Press.

Kobak, R. Rogers, and Cindy Hazan. 1991. *Parents and Spouses: Attachment Strategies and Marital Functioning*. Newark: University of Delaware.

Kobasa, Suzanne C. 1979. "Stressful Life Events, Personality, and Health: An Inquiry into Hardiness." *Journal of Personality and Social Psychology* 37: 1–11.

Kornblith, Hilary. 2002. *Knowledge and Its Place in Nature*. New York: Oxford University Press.

Korsgaard, Christine. 1996. *The Sources of Normativity*. New York: Cambridge University Press.

Kozma, Albert, and Michael J. Stones. 1983. "Predictors of Happiness." *Journal of Gerontology* 38, 5: 626–628.

Kraut, Richard. 1979. "Two Conceptions of Happiness." *The Philosophical Review* 88, 2: 167–197.

———. 2007. *What is Good and Why: The Ethics of Well-Being*. Cambridge, MA: Harvard University Press.

Kringelbach, Morten L., and Kent C. Berridge. 2010. "The Functional Neuroanatomy of Pleasure and Happiness." *Discovery Medicine* 9, 49: 579–589.

Kringelbach, Morten L., and Kent C. Berridge. 2012. "The Joyful Mind." *Scientific American* 307, 2: 40–45.

Kripke, Saul. 1972. *Naming and Necessity*. Hoboken, NJ: Wiley-Blackwell.

Landman, Janet T., and Robyn M. Dawes. 1982. "Smith and Glass' Conclusions Stand Up Under Scrutiny." *American Psychologist* 37: 504–516.

Lavrakas, Paul J., John R. Buri, and Mark S. Mayzner. 1976. "A Perspective on the Recognition of Other Race Faces." *Perception & Psychophysics* 20: 475–481.

Leonhardt, David. 2008. "Maybe Money Does Buy Happiness After All." *New York Times*. April 16, 2008.

Lewis, Kyle, Donald Lange, and Lynette Gillis. 2005. "Transactive Memory Systems, Learning, and Learning Transfer." *Organization Science* 16, 6: 581–598.

Lewontin, Richard C. 1974. *The Genetic Basis of Evolutionary Change*. New York: Columbia University Press.

Liang, D. W., R. Moreland, and L. Argote. 1995. "Group Versus Individual Training and Group Performance: The Mediating Role of Transactive Memory." *Personality and Social Psychology Bulletin* 21, 4: 384–393.

Loewenstein, George. 1994. "The Psychology of Curiosity: A Review and Reinterpretation." *Psychological Bulletin* 116, 1: 75–98.

Loewenstein, George, D. Adler, D. Behrens, and J. Gillins. 1992. "Why Pandora Opened the Box: Curiosity as a Desire for Missing Information." Working Paper. Department of Social and Decision Sciences, Carnegie Mellon University. Pittsburgh, PA.

Lukas, Mark. 2010. "Desire Satisfactionism and the Problem of Irrelevant Desires." *Journal of Ethics and Social Philosophy* 4, 2: 1–24.

Lund, D. A., M. S. Caserta, and M. F. Dimond. 1989. "Impact of Spousal Bereavement on the Subjective Well-Being of Older Adults." In D. A. Lund, ed., *Older Bereaved Spouses: Research with Practical Applications*, 3–15. New York: Hemisphere.

Lykken, David T. 1997. "Happy is as Happy Does." American Psychological Society Presidential Symposium. Washington, DC. May 24, 1997.

Lykken, David T., M. McGue, A. Tellegen, and T. J. Bouchard, Jr. 1992. "Genetic Traits That May Not Run in Families." *American Psychologist* 47, 12: 1565–1577.

Lykken, David T., and Auke Tellegen. 1996. "Happiness is a Stochastic Phenomenon." *Psychological Science* 7, 3: 186–189.

Lyubomirsky, Sonja. 2008. *The How of Happiness: A Scientific Approach to Getting the Life You Want*. New York: Penguin Press.

Lyubomirsky, Sonja, Laura A. King, and Ed Diener. 2005. "The Benefits of Frequent Positive Affect: Does Happiness Lead to Success." *Psychological Bulletin* 131, 6: 803–855.

Lyubomirsky, Sonja, and Kari L. Tucker. 1998. "Implications of Individual Differences in Subjective Happiness for Perceiving, Interpreting, and Thinking About Life Events." *Motivation and Emotion* 22, 2: 155–186.

Machery, Edouard. 2009. *Doing without Concepts*. New York: Oxford University Press.

Magnus, Keith, and Ed Diener. 1991. "A Longitudinal Analysis of Personality, Life Events, and Subjective Well-Being." Paper presented at 63rd Annual Meeting of the Midwestern Psychological Association, Chicago, IL.

Martin, Leslie, Howard S. Friedman, Joan S. Tucker, Carol Tomlinson-Keasey, Michael H. Criqui, and Joseph E. Schwartz. 2002. "A Life

Course Perspective on Childhood Cheerfulness and Its Relation to Mortality Risk." *Personality and Social Psychology Bulletin* 28: 1155–1165.

Meier, Stephan, and Alois Stutzer. 2008. "Is Volunteering Rewarding in Itself?" *Economica* 75: 39–59.

Melton, R. J. 1995. "The Role of Positive Affect in Syllogism Performance." *Personality and Social Psychology Bulletin* 21: 788–794.

Mendola, J. 2006. "Intuitive Hedonism." *Philosophical Studies: An International Journal for Philosophy in the Analytic Tradition* 128, 2: 441–477.

———. 2009. "Real Desires and Well-Being." *Philosophical Issues* 19, 1: 148–165.

Mikulincer, Mario, Victor Florian, and Aron Weller. 1993. "Attachment Styles, Coping Strategies, and Post-Traumatic Psychological Distress: The impact of the Gulf War in Israel." *Journal of Personality and Social Psychology* 64: 817–826.

Mill, John Stuart. 1861/1969. *Utilitarianism.* In J. M. Robson, ed., *Collected Works of John Stuart Mill, Vol. X: Essays on Ethics, Religion, and Society*, 203–259. Toronto: University of Toronto Press.

Moore, G. E. 1903/1993. *Principia Ethica.* Cambridge: Cambridge University Press.

Moos, Rudolf H. 1988. *Coping Response Inventory Manual.* Palo Alto, CA: Stanford University and Department of Veterans Affairs Medical Centers.

Moses, J., Andrew Steptoe, Andrew Mathews, and Sara Edwards. 1989. "The Effects of Exercise Training on Mental Well-Being in the Normal Population: A Controlled Trial." *Journal of Psychosomatic Research* 33, 1: 47–61.

Nesse, Randolph M., and George C. Williams. 1996. *Why We Get Sick: The New Science of Darwinian Medicine.* New York: Vintage.

Nolen-Hoeksema, Susan, Blair E. Wisco, and Sonja Lyubomirsky. 2008. "Rethinking Rumination." *Perspectives on Psychological Science* 3, 5: 400–424.

Nozick, Robert. 1974. *Anarchy, State, and Utopia.* New York: Basic Books.

Nussbaum, Martha C. 2001. *Women and Human Development: The Capabilities Approach.* Cambridge: Cambridge University Press.

Oishi, Shigehiro, Ed Diener, and Richard E. Lucas. 2007. "The Optimum Level of Well-Being: Can People Be Too Happy?" *Perspectives on Psychological Science* 2, 4: 346–360.

Olds, James. 1956. "Pleasure Centers in the Brain." *Scientific American* 195: 105–116.

Overvold, Mark C. 1982. "Self-Interest and Getting What You Want. In H. Miller and W.Williams, eds., *The Limits of Utilitarianism*. Minneapolis, MN: University of Minnesota Press.

Parfit, Derek. 1984. *Reasons and Persons*. New York: Oxford University Press.

———. 2011. *On What Matters*. New York: Oxford University Press.

Penedo, Frank J., and Jason R. Dahn. 2005. "Exercise and Well-Being: A Review of Mental and Physical Health and Benefits Associated with Physical Activity." *Current Opinion in Psychiatry* 18: 189–193.

Peterson, Christopher. 2006. *A Primer in Positive Psychology*. New York: Oxford University Press.

Peterson, Christopher, and Lisa C. Barrett. 1987. "Explanatory Style and Academic Performance Among University Freshmen." *Journal of Personality and Social Psychology* 53: 603–607.

Peterson, Christopher, and Martin E. P. Seligman. 2004. *Character Strengths and Virtues: A Handbook and Classification*. New York: Oxford University Press.

Pinquart, Martin, and Silvia Sörensen. 2000. "Influences of Socioeconomic Status, Social Network, and Competence on Subjective Well-Being in Later Life: A Meta-Analysis." *Psychology and Aging* 15, 2: 187–224.

Pistole, M. Carole. 1989. "Attachment in Adult Romantic Relationships: Style of Conflict Resolution and Relationship Satisfaction." *Journal of Social and Personal Relationships* 6: 505–510.

Portmore, Douglas W. 2007. "Welfare and Posthumous Harm." *American Philosophical Quarterly* 44, 1: 27–38.

Post, S. G. 2005. "Altruism, Happiness, and Health: It's Good to be Good." *International Journal of Behavioral Medicine* 12, 2: 66–77

Putnam, Hilary. 1975. "The Meaning of 'Meaning.'" Reprinted in *Mind, Language and Reality*, 215–271. Cambridge: Cambridge University Press.

Railton, Peter. 2003. "Facts and Values." *Facts, Values, Norms: Essays Towards a Morality of Consequence*. Cambridge: Cambridge University Press.

Rawls, John. 1971. *A Theory of Justice*. Cambridge, MA: Harvard University Press.

Redelmeier, Donald, and Daniel Kahneman. 1996. "Patients' Memories of Painful Medical Treatments: Real-Time and Retrospective Evaluations of Two Minimally Invasive Procedures." *Pain* 66: 3–8.

Roberts, Brent W., Avshalom Caspi, and Terrie E. Moffitt. 2003. "Experiences and Personality Development in Young Adulthood." *Journal of Personality and Social Psychology* 84, 3: 582–593.

Sandvak, Ed, Ed Diener, and Larry Seidlitz. 1993. "Subjective Well-Being: The Convergence and Stability of Self-Report and Non-Self-Report Measures." *Journal of Personality* 61: 317–342.

Scanlon, T. M. 1998a. "The Status of Well-Being." In G. B. Peterson, ed., *The Tanner Lectures on Human Values*, Vol. 19, 91–143. Salt Lake City: The University of Utah Press.

———. 1998b. *What We Owe to Each Other*. Cambridge, MA: The Belknap Press of Harvard University Press.

Schwarz, Norbert, and Fritz Strack. 1999. "Reports of Subjective Well-Being: Judgmental Processes and Their Methodological Implications." In D. Kahneman, E. Diener, and N. Schwarz, eds., *The Foundations of Hedonic Psychology*. New York: Russell Sage Foundation.

Scully, Deirdre, John Kremer, Mary M. Meade, Rodger Graham, and Katrin Dudgeon. 1998. "Physical Exercise and Psychological Well Being: A Critical Review." *Journal of Sports Medicine* 32: 111–120.

Seligman, Martin E. P. 1990. *Learned Optimism: How to Change Your Mind and Your Life*. New York: Random House, Inc.

———. 2007. *What You Can Change and What You Can't: The Complete Guide to Successful Self-Improvement*. New York: Random House, Inc.

Seligman, Martin E. P., and M. Csikszentmihalyi. 2000. "Positive Psychology: An Introduction." *American Psychologist* 55, 1: 5–14.

Seligman, Martin E. P., Susan Nolen-Hoeksema, N. Thornton, and K. M. Thornton. 1990. "Explanatory Style as a Mechanism of Disappointing Athletic Performance." *Psychological Science* 1: 143–146.

Seligman, Martin E. P., and P. Schulman. 1986. "Explanatory Style as a Predictor of Productivity and Quitting among Life Insurance Sales Agents." *Journal of Personality and Social Psychology* 50: 832–838.

Seligman, Martin E. P., Tracy A. Steen, Nansook Park, and Christopher Peterson. 2005. "Empirical Validation of Interventions." *American Psychologist* 60, 5: 410–421.

Sen, Amartya. 1999. *Development as Freedom*. New York: Oxford University Press.

Shapiro, Shauna L., Gary E. R. Schwartz, and Craig Santerre. 2002. "Meditation and Positive Psychology." In C. R. Snyder and S. Lopes, eds.,

Handbook of Positive Psychology, 632–645. Oxford: Oxford University Press.

Simpson, Jeffry A., William S. Rholes, and Julia S. Nelligan. 1992. "Support Seeking and Support Giving within Couples in an Anxiety-Provoking Situation: The Role of Attachment Styles." *Journal of Personality and Social Psychology* 62: 434–446.

Smith, Mary Lee, and Gene V. Glass. 1977. "Meta-Analysis of Psychotherapy Outcome Studies." *American Psychologist* 32: 752–760.

Snyder, C. R., and Shane J. Lopez. 2005. *Handbook of Positive Psychology*. New York: Oxford University Press.

Sober, Elliott. 1988. "Apportioning Causal Responsibility." *The Journal of Philosophy* 85, 6: 303–318.

Sosis, Clifford. 2014. "Hedonic Possibilities and Heritability Statistics." *Philosophical Psychology* 27, 5: 681–702.

Spreitzer, G.M., K. Sutcliffe, J.E. Dutton, S. Sonenshein, and A.M. Grant. 2005. "A Socially Embedded Model of Thriving at Work." *Organization Science* 16, 5: 537–550.

Staw, Barry M., Robert I. Sutton, and Lisa H. Pelled. 1994. "Employee Positive Emotion and Favorable Outcomes at the Workplace." *Organization Science* 5, 1: 51–71.

Stevenson, Betsey, and Justin Wolfers. 2008. "Economic Growth and Subjective Well-Being: Reassessing the Easterlin Paradox." *Brookings Papers on Economic Activity* 39, 1: 1–102.

Stich, Stephen. 1983. *From Folk Psychology to Cognitive Science*. Cambridge, MA: MIT Press.

Stone, A. A., S. S. Shiffman, and M. W. DeVries. 1999. "Ecological Momentary Assessment." In D. Kahneman, E. Diener, and N. Schwartz, eds., *Well-Being: The Foundations of Hedonic Psychology*, 26–39. New York: Russell Sage Foundation.

Stones, Michael J., and A. Kozma. 1991. "A Magical Model of Happiness." *Social Indicators Research* 25, 1: 31–50.

Strack, Fritz, Norbert Schwarz, and Elisabeth Gschneidinger. 1985. "Happiness and Reminiscing: The Role of Time Perspective, Mood, and Mode of Thinking." *Journal of Personality and Social Psychology* 49: 1460–1469.

Stutzer, Alois, and Bruno S. Frey. 2008. "Stress that Doesn't Pay: The Commuting Paradox." *The Scandinavian Journal of Economics* 110, 2: 339–366.

Sumner, L. W. 1996. *Welfare, Happiness, and Ethics*. New York: Oxford University Press.

Sumner, L. W. 2000. "Something in Between." In R. Crisp and B. Hooker, eds., *Wellbeing and Morality: Essays in Honour Of James Griffin*, 1–19. New York: Oxford University Press.

Swanton, Christine. 2003. *Virtue Ethics: A Pluralistic View*. New York: Oxford University Press.

Teasdale, John D. 1988. "Cognitive Vulnerability to Persistent Depression." *Cognition and Emotion* 2: 247–274.

Tellegen, A., David T. Lykken, Thomas J. Bouchard Jr., Kimerly J. Wilcox, Nancy L. Segal, and Stephen Rich. 1988. "Personality Similarity in Twins Reared Apart and Together." *Journal of Personality and Social Psychology* 54, 6: 1031–1039.

Thoits, Peggy A., and Lyndi N. Hewitt. 2001. "Volunteer Work and Well-Being." *Journal of Health and Social Behavior* 42, 2: 115–131.

Tiberius, Valerie. 2004. "Cultural Differences and Philosophical Accounts of Well-Being." *Journal of Happiness Studies* 5: 293–314.

———. 2006. "Well-Being: Psychological Research for Philosophers." *Philosophy Compass* 1, 5: 493–505.

———. 2008. *The Reflective Life: Living Wisely with Our Limits*. Oxford: Oxford University Press.

———. 2014. "Beyond The Experience Machine: How to Build a Theory of Well-being." In M. C. Haug, ed., *Philosophical Methodology: The Armchair or The Laboratory*, 398–415. New York: Routledge Publishing.

Trout, J. D. 2009. *The Empathy Gap: Building Bridges to the Good Life and the Good Society*. New York: Penguin Group Inc.

Watson, David, Lee Ann Clark, and Auke Tellegen. 1988. "Development and Validation of Brief Measures of Positive and Negative Affect: The PANAS Scales." *Journal of Personality and Social Psychology* 54: 1063–1070.

Werner, Emmy E. 1983. "Resilience and Recovery Findings from the Kauai Longitudinal Study." *Research, Policy and Practice in Children's Mental Health* 19, 1: 11–14.

Wilson, Warner R. 1967. "Correlates of Avowed Happiness." *Psychological Bulletin* 67, 4: 294–306.

Wilson, Timothy, Daniel T. Gilbert, and David B. Centerbar. 2002. "Making Sense: The Causes of Emotional Evanescence." In I. Brocas and J. Carrillo, eds., *The Psychology of Economic Decisions. Vol. 1: Rationality and Well-Being*, 209–233. New York: Oxford University Press.

Wortman, Camille B., and Roxane Cohen Silver. 1989. "The Myths of Coping with Loss." *Journal of Consulting and Clinical Psychology* 57: 349–357.

Wright, Thomas A., and Douglas G. Bonnet. 1997. "The Contribution of Burnout to Work Performance." *Journal of Organizational Behavior* 18: 491–499.

Wright, Thomas A., Douglas G. Bonett, and Dennis A. Sweeney. 1993. "Mental Health and Work Performance: Results of a Longitudinal Study." *Journal of Occupational and Organizational Psychology* 66: 277–284.

Wright, Thomas A., and Russell Cropanzano. 2000. "Psychological Well-Being and Job Satisfaction as Predictors of Job Performance." *Journal of Occupational Health Psychology* 5, 1: 84–94.

Wright, Beatrice A., and Shane J. Lopez 2005. "Widening the Diagnostic Focus: A Case for Including Human Strengths and Environmental Resources." In C. R. Snyder and S. J. Lopez, eds., *Handbook of Positive Psychology*. New York: Oxford University Press.

INDEX

Note: Locators followed by the letter 'n' refer to notes.

adaptation, evolutionary, 37–9
adaptation, hedonic, 157–65, 167,
    168 n.3, 170, 172, 181–2
adaptive preferences, 131, 157–9
affect-stabilizing mechanisms,
    161–2, 164–5, 177
Alexandrova, Anna, 33, 166
altruism, 89–90
Aristotelianism, 2–3, 28–9, 48,
    57–8, 111, 138–47, 188,
    192–3
authentic happiness theory, 111,
    129–38, 160, 165
    reality requirement, 131–2
    full information requirement,
    131–5

Baron, Robert A., 69–70
Batholomew, Kim, 78–9
basic respect assumption, 15–19
Bem, Daryl, J., 178–9
Bentham, Jeremy, 147, 166
Berridge, Kent C., 43, 121–2

Biswas-Diener, Robert, 146–7,
    156–7
Boyd, Richard N., 40, 198–9, 206
Branigan, Christine, 88–89
Broaden and Build Hypothesis,
    36–9, 75, 79
Bukstel, Lee H., 158

Calcutta Study, 156–7
Caspi, Avshalom, 82–3, 98, 178–9
Centerbar, David B., 161–2, 165
character strengths project, 142–6
Cooper, Harris, 71
coping, 88
Costa, Paul, 71–2, 88
Crisp, Roger, 23, 27, 112, 114,
    121
curiosity, 9, 47–9, 92–3
cycle, 8–11, 66
    altruism and happiness, 89–90
    anxiety-misinterpretation, 97
    broaden-and-build, 36–9
    curiosity-knowledge, 92–3

cycle (*continued*)
 depressive, 11, 97–8
 engagement and positive
  affect, 88–9
 happiness-success, 36–7, 81–3
 healthy coping and positive
  affect, 88
 optimism and success, 86–7
 positive affect-friendliness,
  68–9
 positive affect-others judge
  one more positively, 70–1
 positive affect-successful
  relationships, 76–7
 positive professional success, 9
 relationship-relationship skills,
  77–9

Darwall, Stephen, 139, 141,
 198 n.1
De Brigard, Felipe, 117
Deaton, Angus, 118
DeNeve, Kristina M., 71
desire satisfaction, 27–8, 122–3,
 125, 126–8
Descriptive Adequacy, 20–3
Diener, Ed, 36, 48, 71, 76–7,
 81–2, 88, 149–50, 153–4,
 156–9, 171, 188
Duncker's Candle Task, 85–6
duration neglect, 167–8, 169 n.4
dysthymia, 11

Elder, Glen H., 178–9
emotional state view of happiness, 150–1
emotional well-being, 118–19,
 120–1, 128
eudaimonia, 138, 146
exercise, 98–9

experience machine, 22–3, 27–30,
 113–17, 187
extraversion, 67, 71–4, 80

Feldman, Fred, 166–7, 190–1
fitting problem, 110
 and hedonism, 117–19
 and informed desire theory,
  126–9
 and network theory, 111
Fredrickson, Barbara L., 9–10,
 36–9, 75, 79, 88–9, 91
friendship network, 67–74, 84

genetic determination, 170–80
Gilbert, Daniel T., 161–2, 165
Griffin, James, 20, 27, 28, 58,
 115, 123, 125, 152
Griffiths, Paul E., 32, 33–4

happiness. *See* authentic happiness
  theory; emotional state view
  of happiness; objective
  happiness; placeholder view
  of happiness
Harker, Lee Anne, 77
Haybron, Daniel M., 18, 33, 136,
 137, 150, 152, 176
Hazan, Cindy, 77, 78, 79
Headey, Bruce, 72–4, 77, 84, 88,
 170, 171
hedonic hotspots, 121–2
hedonic set points. *See* set point
 theory
hedonic treadmill, 164
hedonism, 2–3, 27, 111–22, 127,
 140, 147, 187, 188, 192–3
heritability, 171–8
Hewitt, Lyndi N., 90
hindsight bias, 59–60

homeostatic property clusters, 40–1, 43–4, 45, 56–7, 198
homogeneity hypothesis, 176–80
Horowitz, Leonard, 78
Hume, David, 202. *See also under* rationality

ill-being, 96–101, 182
inclusive approach, 1–2, 4–5, 14–34, 43, 108, 141, 146–8, 150, 196
  and Aristotelianism, 138–9
  and authentic happiness theory, 129, 135–6
  and hedonism, 112, 117, 119
  and informed desire theory, 124
  and network theory, 43, 62–3, 147–8, 161, 180–1, 184–5, 192, 194, 201, 208–9
inclusive good, 193
informed desire theory, 2–3, 27–8, 111, 122–9, 188, 192–3
informed desires, 28, 123–5, 126–9
Isen, Alice M., 68, 85–6, 90

Johnson, Kareem J., 91
Joiner, Thomas, 88

Kahneman, Daniel, 118, 166–70, 181
Kashdan, Todd B., 146–7
Keltner, Dacher, 77
Kilmann, Peter R., 158
King, Laura A., 36, 71, 146–7, 171
Kringelbach, Morten L., 43, 121–2

life satisfaction, 71–2, 118–19, 137, 153–4, 157–8, 162–3
Lucas, Richard E., 48, 81–2, 154, 158
Lukas, Mark, 27–8, 125
Lund, Dale A., 158
Lykken, David T., 170–1, 173–4, 176
Lyubomirsky, Sonja, 36, 69, 71, 97, 149–50, 171

Machery, Edouard, 32
McCrae, Robert R., 71–2, 88
Meno's Paradox, 14–15
Moffitt, Terrie E., 82–3
Moore, G. E., 199

negative (vicious) causal network, 11, 41, 96–8
  dynamics, 96–101
network
  friendship (*see* friendship network)
  professional success (*see* professional and academic success network)
  relationship (*see* relationship network)
network theory of well-being, 8, 10–13, 44–5, 47, 57–8, 66, 93, 101–2, 105–6, 169–70. *See also* positive causal network (PCN), robustness; positive causal network fragment (PCN fragment)
norm of reaction, 174–5
normative consilience thesis, 140
normativity, 196–9
normativity requirement, 196–207

normativity requirement (*continued*)
  meaning demand, 199–201
  motivation demand, 202–5, 206
    normal person motivation
      demand, 205, 206
    rational motivation demand,
      204–5
    unrestricted motivation
      demand, 203–4
  objective reason demand, 201–2
Nozick, Robert, 27, 113–16, 143
Nun Study, 51–3

objective happiness, 166–70, 181
objective list theory, 57–8
open-question argument, 199–200
optimism, 9, 49, 80, 86–7
ordinization mechanisms, 162–3
Overvold, Mark C., 28, 125
Own Race Bias, 91

panic attacks, 96–7
Park, Nansook, 99–101
Pelled, Lisa H., 83–5
Peterson, Christopher, 48–9, 78–9,
  87, 99–101, 142–5, 156
Pinquart, Martin, 80
placeholder view of happiness,
  149–52, 168
Plato, 126, 202
pleasure, 118–22
positive affect, 48, 55–6, 75, 79,
  80, 118, 140, 154
  cycles involving, 37–9, 67–72,
    76–7, 88–92
positive causal network (PCN),
  39–44
positive causal network (PCN),
  dynamics, 93–101
  causal drivers, 43–5, 50–1,
    53–8, 95–6, 188

enhancers, 95–6
promoters, 95–9
essentials, 94–5, 97–8
prerequisites, 94–5, 99
positive causal network (PCN),
  robustness, 45–51, 82,
    94–6, 186–9, 191
  Intensity, 48–50
  Size, 51
positive causal network (PCN),
  interpersonal, 101–4, 211
positive causal network fragment
  (PCN fragment), 10, 11–12,
    53–8, 85–93, 102–3, 169–70,
    187, 191, 196, 209
Positive Organization Scholarship,
  103. *See also* positive causal
  network (PCN), interpersonal
Positive Psychology, 4–6, 35–6,
  53–4, 59–107, 110–11, 146,
  149–51, 154, 170, 181–2,
  210–11
  and authentic happiness
    theory, 137–8
  characterizations, 4, 61–2, 64–6
  foundation problem, 4–5
  and hedonism, 117–22
  and informed desire theory,
    126–9
  and moralized views of
    well-being, 141–6
privileging problem, 110–11
  and hedonism, 119–22
  and informed desire theory, 128
  and network theory, 111, 154
professional and academic
  success network, 79–85

rationality, accounts of
  means-end (Humean), 204–5
  non-Humean, 205

recalibration mechanisms, 161, 162–5
relationship network, 74–9, 84–5
remote desires, 27–8, 125
Ring of Gyges, 202
Roberts, Brent W., 82–3
rumination, 97

Satisfaction with Life Scale, 153–4
Scanlon, Thomas M., 54, 185, 192–6, 201
Schwarz, Norbert, 155–6, 162–3
Scollon, Christie N., 154, 158
Seligman, Martin E. P., 4, 9, 48–9, 62, 76–7, 78–9, 86–7, 88, 98–101, 142–5, 149, 171
sensible knave, 202–4
set point theory, 170–80
Shaver, Philip, 77, 78, 79
shyness, 178–9
Silver, Roxane Cohen, 157–8
Solomonic strategy, 31–2
Sörensen, Silvia, 80
Spreitzer, Gretchen M., 103–4
Staw, Barry M., 83–5
Steen, Tracy A., 99–101
Strack, Fritz, 155–6, 162–3
Subjective Well-Being (SWB), 153–9
Sumner, Leonard W., 20–2, 129–38, 150
Sutton, Robert I., 83–5

Tellegen, Auke, 154, 170–1, 173–4, 176
Thoits, Peggy A., 90
Tiberius, Valerie, 21, 25, 33, 129, 135, 137–8, 181

traditional approach, 20–34, 140–1, 146 n.1
Descriptive Adequacy, 20–3
Insulation Thesis, 24
Philosophy First, 20, 24–5
Vulnerability Thesis, 24
traditional approach, problems, 26–30
diversity challenge, 20, 30
epistemological problem, 26–30
stalemate problem, 1, 3–5, 26–30, 140–1, 146, 147–8, 160–1

upward spirals, 36, 209. *See also* positive causal network (PCN)

virtue, 48, 138–46
volunteer work, 90, 140

Wearing, Alexander, 72–4, 77, 84, 88, 170
well-being, degrees of, 10–12, 57, 102, 116, 139, 140, 146, 186–9, 191
well-being, of groups. *See* positive causal network (PCN), interpersonal
well-being, theories of. *See* Aristotelianism; authentic happiness theory; hedonism; informed desire theory; network theory; objective list theory
Wilson, Timothy, 161–2, 165
work, 79–85
Wortman, Camille B., 157–8

Yearbook Study, 77

Objective: To examine whether regular exercise is associated with anxiety, depression and personality in a large population-based sample as a function of gender and age

Methods:

CPSIA information can be obtained at www.ICGtesting.com
Printed in the USA
BVOW08s1934120816

458887BV00003B/9/P